Lessons and Laughter from Life's Amusing Adventures

By

Tony Moceri

Copyright © 2024 by James "Tony" Moceri

Published by Skinny Brown Dog Media
Atlanta, GA / Punta del Este, Uruguay

All rights reserved. No part of this book may be reproduced in any form or by any electronic or mechanical means, including information storage and retrieval systems, without permission in writing from the publisher, except by a reviewer who may quote brief passages in a review.

Skinny Brown Dog Media supports copyright. Copyright fuels creativity, encourages diverse voices, promotes free speech, and creates a vibrant culture. Thank you for buying an authorized edition of this book and for complying with copyright laws by not reproducing, scanning, or distributing any part of it in any form without permission. You are supporting writers and allowing Skinny Brown Dog Media to continue to publish books for readers like you.

For Information, Contact:
Distributed by Skinny Brown Dog Media
SkinnyBrownDogMedia.com
Email: Info@SkinnyBrownDogMedia.com

A Wandering Mind
Lessons and Laughter from Life's Amusing Adventures
Tony Moceri
Tony@tonymoceri.com
https://tonymoceri.com

Library of Congress Cataloging-in-Publication Data
ISBN eBook: 978-1-965235-32-4
ISBN Paperback: 978-1-965235-06-5
ISBN Dust Jacket Cloth Cover Hardback: 978-1-965235-04-1
ISBN Case Laminate: 978-1-965235-05-8

To *Lindsey* and *Harper,*

Thank you for living with my Wandering Mind.

TABLE OF CONTENTS

01. They Can't Say Yes if You Don't Ask ... 19
02. Rejection ... 23
03. It's Not in the Magazine? ... 25
04. Giving Writing Meaning ... 31
05. Back to Western ... 35
06. Cold Pizza ... 39
07. Lost ... 43
08. Dexterous and Deft ... 45
09. Designing Life ... 47
10. Sitting Duck ... 53
11. 1% Infinity ... 55
12. Get Up ... 59
13. Get Better ... 61
14. Balance ... 63
15. Working in Bursts ... 69
16. The Walking Meeting ... 73
17. The 30-Minute Walk ... 75
18. Walk ... 77
19. Feel Sick Act Sick ... 79
20. Road Tripping ... 83
21. Van Lessons ... 87
22. Top Speed ... 91
23. Naming Fiji ... 97
24. Fiji ... 101

25. Selling Gretta and Picking up Maui 105
26. Lessons Learned: 1987 VW Vanagon 115
27. Camping in the Rain 119
28. Chilin With Milly 123
29. Don't Trust Wikipedia 127
30. Hazel 135
31. Creativity 139
32. Creativity 141
33. Break Routine to Get Creative 145
34. Playtime 147
35. Play 151
36. Yard Game Nation 153
37. Games 161
38. Bubble Wrap 163
39. Luck 167
40. Get Educated 169
41. Youth Sports 179
42. More Than Basketball 187
43. Feeding the Cows 191
44. Conversate 197
45. How's the Weather? 199
    Afterword 203
    About the Author 205
    Appendix A: 'Quotes' 207

Foreword

Tony and I have known each other for as long as two people can remember. Throughout our shared history, I've watched Tony pursue his wandering mind, stringing together adventures, tender moments, and endless learning, all with a backdrop of fun.

While Tony has chosen to share some monumental tales here, each story is underpinned by a balance of whimsy and intention. Behind his playful pursuit of creativity and togetherness lies a foundation of tough questions and focused planning, enabling the spontaneous life he now enjoys.

This book doesn't offer a step-by-step guide to getting your life together—Tony wouldn't presume to tell you how to improve your life. Only you can do that. As the Oracle at Delphi said, "Know Thyself." Easier said than done. Tony's advice, woven through these stories, can help fill in the gaps as you embark on your journey of self-discovery.

The book is perfectly broken up into easy-to-read stories and poems, offering much to its readers. Tony shares tales of building a rewarding, fulfilling life with low stress, though the stories themselves can be stress-inducing. Who wants a line of irate drivers behind them when they're powerless to do anything about it? Tony's advice for such situations—and many more—will resonate with anyone learning to take life less seriously.

I admire the clarity and perspective Tony brings to each story, consistently highlighting the journey's value, the importance of responsibility, and how our relationships define us. His stories prompt reflection and introspection, and even during tear-jerking moments, Tony's humor shines through, offering much-needed laughter.

Upon completing the book, I felt fortunate to know someone spreading such a positive message and to count Tony among my closest friends. We have an amazing opportunity to live in the moment and make our chosen impact on the world. Tony has given us a gift with this book, showing us an inspiring example of a life well-lived. I hope you find it as enjoyable and helpful as I do.

Zachary Graham

July 2024

A Guide to Read and Digest "A Wandering Mind"

As someone who has come to intimately know Tony Moceri's... unique thought process (and I use that term extremely loosely), through editing and assembling this collection, I feel obligated to provide you with this guide.

01. Buckle up and embrace the ride: Get ready to dive headfirst into the whimsical world of Tony's mind. It's like a literary amusement park, full of twists, turns, and unexpected bursts of laughter. Keep your hands and feet inside the vehicle at all times, and prepare for a wild journey!

02. Savor the flavors: Think of each essay, story, or poem as a delectable treat for your brain. Don't just gobble them up like a hungry hippo; take your time to relish every morsel of wit and wisdom. If a particular piece really tickles your fancy, feel free to do a happy dance and reread it to your heart's content.

03. Play the "Relate and Reflect" game: As you navigate through Tony's experiences and insights, try to spot the similarities to your own life. It's like a cosmic game of "Where's Waldo?" but instead of finding a bespectacled, striped-shirt-wearing fellow, you're uncovering your own hidden truths and revelations.

04. Embrace the variety pack: "A Wandering Mind" is like a literary smorgasbord, offering a little something for

everyone. It's okay if some pieces resonate with you more than others – that's just your brain's way of saying, "Ooh, this one's my favorite flavor!" Embrace the eclectic mix and enjoy the buffet of thoughts and ideas.

05. Laugh until your abs hurt: Tony's humor is like a secret ingredient that makes everything better. Don't be afraid to let out a guffaw, a chuckle, or even a snort (if you're feeling extra sassy). Laughter is the best medicine, and "A Wandering Mind" is your prescription for a healthy dose of hilarity.

06. Start a brain-sharing bonanza: Once you've had your fill of Tony's mental escapades, it's time to spread the joy. Grab your friends, family, or unsuspecting strangers and start a lively discussion about your favorite pieces. It's like a book club, but with more laughter and less pretentious cheese platters.

07. Revisit and marinate: After you've finished the book, let the ideas and insights marinate in your mind for a bit. Revisit the pieces that made you go, "Whoa, that's deep!" and let them percolate in your brain. It's like a mental spa day, where you get to soak in the brilliance of Tony's wandering mind.

08. Put the "fun" in "life lessons": Take the wisdom and insights you've gleaned from "A Wandering Mind" and apply them to your own life in a way that makes you smile. Embrace your inner child, find joy in the simple things, and don't be afraid to color outside the lines. After all, life's too short to be a stick-in-the-mud!

So, there you have it – your guide to reading and digesting "A Wandering Mind" without taking yourself too seriously. Remember, this book is intended for nothing more than looking at that wild, wonderful, and sometimes wacky adventure called life.

Introduction

Thank you for taking the time to sit down with my book. Completing this book has been a lengthy process. Some pieces were written years ago, and some are new. I always wanted to write a book, often starting the process, but I always hit mental roadblocks. Having so much to say on one topic is not really how I'm wired. I have many interests and enjoy wandering through different areas. This book reflects that, and I hope it also reflects the journey involved in its creation. While I am now seen as a writer by those who have read my other work, growing up, the thought of me being a writer was somewhat laughable.

Describing me as a challenging, or maybe just an exhausting child, would be accurate. I wasn't a total deviant, although I had my moments, but I simply had a lot of energy. I remember my mom setting a timer on the stove when I was supposed to be doing homework. A thin knob stuck out from the face of the oven, and it turned past each minute like a clock. I would stare at that little knob, waiting for it to release the ding as though I was using the Force. She hoped it would get me to sit still for fifteen straight minutes. This felt like an eternity to me. If she made the mistake of leaving the room, I would race over and turn the timer subtly towards zero, shaving off a minute or two before scurrying back to my stool at the counter where I pretended to do my work. At school, I had a hard time sitting still and couldn't figure out why I wasn't supposed to talk to everyone around me. I treated school like social hour, which resulted in a lot of time spent in the hallway.

In addition to being overly energetic, my spelling was abysmal, and my approach to punctuation and grammar was to place symbols randomly into the text in hopes of getting lucky. Honestly, I still can't spell, and many punctuation and grammar rules are a mystery to me. Fortunately, now there's an app for that, along with helpful editors. Somehow my mom and teachers got me through elementary school and junior high and into high school. My freshman year of high school, I had the good fortune of having Ms. Pitts as my English teacher. Ms. Pitts took none of my crap. She quickly moved my seat to the front, right by her, and while other kids changed seats throughout the year, I stayed put. For the entire year, and again my junior year, Ms. Pitts had me front and center, crippling my ability to distract myself and the rest of the class.

When I arrived in Ms. Pitts's class, I was a poor reader and struggled with the idiosyncrasies of writing, although I always had a lot to say. During those years with Ms. Pitts, she introduced me to J.D. Salinger and John Steinbeck, changing my perception of reading. She covered my writing in red ink, telling me that the ink represented love, not blood, although I'm sure there were times in class when she would have loved to inflict a little pain on me. The incredible thing is she didn't just do this for me. She poured this effort into student after student for her entire career, shaping the lives of so many young people. Out of the challenges I faced as a student trying to figure out how letters and words went together, and she faced trying to educate me, a friendship was formed. I am pleased to say that to this day, LaLani Pitts and I are still friends and communicate regularly.

Now that I have a child of my own and have spent decades working with youth in various ways, I understand what a challenge I must have been. Somehow my mom, dad, LaLani, and a village of other adults kept me on track enough to get into college. I majored in history and minored in English, two reading and writing-intensive majors. Reading and writing are both still challenging on many levels, but through it all, I gained a passion for both. It is a good reminder that we have the ability to turn our weaknesses into strengths, and that just because the aptitude isn't naturally there for something doesn't mean it can't be cultivated.

I have included this foundational information in the foreword as a notice to temper expectations. I am not a wordsmith, and I don't necessarily write conventionally. I write what comes to mind, and it comes out as it comes out. I do go back through to edit and do some light rewriting, but that's it. The process of extensive rewriting makes me feel claustrophobic, and I would rather throw a piece of writing out than completely change it. I want my voice to come through and to show those out there who struggle with writing that it's okay to just write how you write. Don't get me wrong, I love reading the work of great writers, but just because they exist doesn't mean there isn't room for the rest of us to write too. There is value in those thoughts and stories being put onto paper.

Through the actual process of getting this book published, my publisher/editor Eric tried very hard to help me improve my writing in general, and the pieces contained within these pages. He gave me thoughts and direction, putting the power in my fingertips to rework the writing. He also gave me resources to help me work on my writing and storytelling skills. While I did dig back into the pages, expanding on some elements, this book is not as polished as Eric, and I'm sure most publishers, would like. I refused to change anything that would change my voice or give the perception that my writing ability is something it's not. While this probably frustrated him to no end, I appreciate that he accepted me and my writing for what we are and didn't bail on me.

So, what might you find on the pages to come? Hopefully, you will find entertainment, humor, inspiration, and insight. My goal was to create a book that shared some of the lessons I have learned over the years. There are original stories and poems by me and quotes by others. They are all meant to complement each other, not just in expressing what I have learned but laying it out there in a way that can be remembered and put into action. Obviously, you can read this book however you want, or drop it in one of those free libraries on the street corner, but what I envisioned was someone spending a handful of minutes with it at a time. I sized the book so that it can slip into a bag or be stuck in a back pocket and used for a bit of entertainment when the social media feed has become tiresome, or tragedy has struck, and your phone battery died.

With that, if you haven't already given up, it's time to start wandering around.

A Note on Quotes

I am a fan of quotes. An efficient quote can say so much in so few words. They are often clichéd and overused, but many are brilliant. They may reflect an insightful mind or someone saying powerful words needed in a moment. Wherever they come from, this small cluster of letters can be more impactful than pages and pages in a book.

That being said, the other thing about quotes is that they are said by humans, which is a bit of a problem for me. Yes, there are great quotes by great people, but there are also great quotes by not-so-good people. As long as someone is alive, no matter how impressive they seem, they have the opportunity to prove otherwise. So, if great words come out of a not-so-great person, does that make the words any less impactful? Can we not learn and use those wise words even if the person was hypocritical in saying them? I think we can, but I am not interested in glamorizing the individual, only the words. I don't want the actions of that person to influence the power of what they once said.

Because of my struggle with humans constantly doing stupid things, I questioned whether or not to include quotes. I feared that putting in a quote by someone whose character is in question or may be damaged in the future would hurt the book's message. I decided to include quotes throughout the book where I think they add to the message I'm trying to get across or, in many cases, say it better than I am able to. It will not say who said them. In Appendix A, the quotes are listed with the person who said them in the order they appear.

If you don't go after what you want, you'll never have it. If you don't ask, the answer is always no. If you don't step forward, you're always in the same place.

The most effective way to do it, is to do it.

01

THEY CAN'T SAY YES IF YOU DON'T ASK

In college, I heard a story about a student who asked girls out every day on campus. His ability to handle rejection was unparalleled. Despite facing rejection after rejection, this guy went on more dates than anyone else. One day, his roommate in the dorm asked why he asked out so many girls and how he managed the rejections. The guy simply said, "It doesn't matter how many no's I get, what matters is that one yes."

While I don't know if this is a true story or an urban legend, what I do know is that there is a good lesson in it. I never mustered the courage to walk around Western Washington University getting shot down, but it's something I think about when facing the possibility of rejection.

Think about how often you've denied yourself opportunities simply because you didn't ask. We are so scared of rejection that we would rather deny ourselves than ask and see what happens. Looking back, I have fallen into this trap throughout my life, and I don't think it was for a good reason. There have been times when I have put myself out there and applied for a job or asked to be involved in something, and I have received a lot of yeses. I'm sure I have also received a lot of no's, but the reality is that I don't remember that many of them. Perhaps it's partly because I have a poor memory, but it's also because it was not some traumatic event. I asked, they said "no," and nothing in my world changed.

I understand that the "no" can be terrifying, and that rejection can feel as though it is actual physical pain, but we have to understand that it is all mental. The reality of the scenario is that the no's we receive will be nothing more than a passing moment. The discomfort will pass, and the no will fade, becoming a distant memory.

Most of the no's I remember were not just no's but were "no, buts." I have found these to be just as good or even better. For example, when I applied for the head track coach position at Mt. Baker High School, Lindsey sent me the position, and I figured since I loved coaching, why not. I had no experience coaching track and, at that point, did not even have any high school coaching experience. So, being unqualified for the position would be an accurate description. On top of that, it turned out that one of the other applicants was highly qualified, and he was a shoo-in for the position. The hiring team made the right decision and gave me a "no." However, they also gave me a "but." That "but" was, would I consider being an assistant coach? Without hesitation, I said yes, and frankly, it could not have turned out better. I loved being an assistant track coach, and it has led to many other coaching opportunities since. My point here is that by not fearing the no, I ended up with a yes, and in hindsight, a better yes for me than what I had been seeking out.

Getting into writing was another instance where I just had to stick my neck out there and go for it. I had dipped my toes in the writing water by writing a blog, but for years I had not been comfortable reaching beyond that point. While I was putting my writing out there into the world, there was no risk of getting a no. People could choose to read it or not, but no one had to approve it. When Covid came along, and I was stuck sitting at home, I decided I would put myself out there as a freelance writer. To my surprise, I got some yeses, and all it took was me asking. This simple step of reaching out to publications led to years of writing opportunities. Through people seeing my work, and the confidence to reach out to other publications, I have had the opportunity to tell stories important to me.

Now it's your turn to go get that yes. What opportunities are passing you by because you're not asking? Would a no really be that detrimental? If there is one thing I have learned, it is that we have no idea what tomorrow will bring. Life is too unpredictable to fear a no. If there is something you want to do, go after it and see what happens. You might get a no, and that's okay because you might get that yes you were looking for. The one thing that is certain is you won't get the yes if you don't ask.

> *I take rejection as someone blowing a bugle in my ear to wake me up and get going, rather than retreat.*

> *So don't you worry your pretty, little mind. People throw rocks at things that shine*

02

REJECTION

Rejection can be a scary thing,
What anxiety it can bring.
Never knowing what could be,
Ask the question, just to see.

Opportunities may pass you by,
Unless you choose to give it a try.
The worst outcome is a 'no,'
And with that, you'll still grow.

The process may create some stress,
But what if they come back with 'yes'?
Now you've done it, you're on your way,
Because you tried, you made your day.

With your fear now overcome,
Your life can beat to your own drum.

> *You may be disappointed if you fail but you are doomed if you don't try*

> *We must accept finite disappointment, but never lose infinite hope*

03

IT'S NOT IN THE MAGAZINE?

Entering the world of freelance writing, I was utterly clueless. Even after four years, I often feel like I'm still faking it. Initially, I didn't talk to anyone about it, nor did I research the profession. Typically, when I get into something new, I educate myself extensively, but this time, I simply dove in. This approach has allowed my writing opportunities to continually expand, though I've been learning on the fly.

Much of my learning has been about the craft of writing, interviewing, and photography, but also about the business side of writing itself. In typical business transactions, two parties agree on a price and exchange money upon completion of the work. Sometimes, money changes hands even before the work begins. Freelance writing, however, operates on a completely different set of rules. While dealings with publications like Whatcom Talk, Business Pulse, and website content are straightforward—if I do this, I get paid—other publications are less predictable. My first eye-opener was with the Mt. Baker Experience.

I had pitched them an article titled 'My Private Island,' about a day my family and I spent paddleboarding to an island on

Diablo Lake in the North Cascades. I was thrilled they liked my idea and told everyone that my story would appear in the summer issue of the magazine. This free publication, popular in our corner of the world for its adventurous tales and great pictures, was something I looked forward to being part of. As the publication date neared, I continually checked local spots where I usually picked up the magazine. When the day came, I eagerly searched for my article but to no avail. After thoroughly searching the magazine forward and backward, I realized my story was not there. Disappointed, I emailed the editor. He informed me that the photos weren't suitable for print but that the story would be published online, and I would still be compensated. Though it felt like a consolation prize, I appreciated both gestures. (I'm happy to report that I'm now a regular contributor to Mt. Baker Experience's print version). I was disappointed but not entirely surprised as photography has never been my strength, though I am improving as I take more photos for my articles. The pictures I had were just casual shots from our day, not specifically taken for an article.

Determined to prevent this from happening again, I became more vigilant about communicating with editors about their expectations for articles, both in writing and photos. If I had them, I started sending photographs ahead of time for approval before I even wrote the article. I felt confident about my place in the writing world, having become consistent with multiple publications and regularly creating blog posts and website copy for businesses. I had reached the point where I assumed that if I wrote it, it would be published. However, this was a good reminder never to get too comfortable.

I discovered American West Magazine on LinkedIn, a publication focusing on stories about the Western States, primarily travel and outdoor activities. This seemed like a perfect match. Lindsey and I love traveling and staying active, so having stories to write and photos to take seemed ideal. I also aspired to be published in Sunset Magazine someday, believing that contributing to American West would be a good step toward building my resume. Despite reaching out to Sunset, I have yet to hear back, but I'll keep trying.

I connected with the editor of American West, and we agreed on an article about camping at Union Creek Campground in Oregon. Excited to be featured in another publication, I eagerly awaited the issue. When it arrived, my concise 450-word story about this fantastic camping spot was there. I was thrilled to be included and to have another platform for my writing. When the next pitch cycle came, I proposed a story about road tripping up the Oregon Coast, focusing on historical bridges and viewpoints. After fine-tuning the details, we agreed on the approach. I sent the photos ahead of time, and everything seemed set. However, prior to publication I received an email stating there wasn't room in the issue for my story.

This was, to say the least, disappointing. I was excited about being featured again and had invested significant effort to meet the expected parameters. Typically, I write in a conversational first-person style, but this time, I crafted a more descriptive piece as requested. Though it felt less natural, I enjoyed the challenge. Ultimately, being told there was no room likely meant it wasn't good enough, which I can accept, though it's not the outcome I desired. Moreover, I wasn't paid for this work, reinforcing the reality that in freelance writing, you are only paid for published pieces. Essentially, you pitch an idea, write the article, and if they like it, you receive a modest payment. Freelance writing isn't a path to wealth; it's about doing what you love and feeling fortunate to be compensated for it.

I don't want this to sound like a complaint.

Since my first payment from Whatcom Talk, I've been amazed that anyone would pay me for my writing. I cherish being able to earn from something I passionately enjoy. I've learned a tremendous amount, had wonderful experiences, and met incredible people through writing. I plan to write for the rest of my life. While rejection is painful and disappointing, it likely serves to ensure I'm continually sharpening my skills—pun intended.

Learning about this new industry has been fascinating. Being perpetually on the cusp of freelancing makes each published article thrilling, akin to flipping a house but with less risk. The writing profession is not for the faint of heart. Each pitch cycle presents a new chance for rejection, there's no standard pay rate, and the ever-present "sorry, we didn't have room" factor looms large.

> *When asked, "How do you write?" I invariably answer, "One word at a time."*

> *Follow your passion. It will lead you to your purpose*

04

GIVING WRITING MEANING

When I began writing articles, I had no clue where my writing would lead. I knew very little about the freelance writing world. People would ask me what type of writing I did, and I would respond that I was open to writing just about anything; I relished the opportunity to get published and build my portfolio. What I slowly realized was that the type of writing wasn't the important part for me. I was writing about businesses, athletes, outdoor recreation, yard games, events, artists, and various other subjects. My enjoyment stemmed not from the subject matter itself, but from my connection to it. Initially, I thought I would understand this connection beforehand, but that has not been the case. Delving into an article can mean a variety of things. Sometimes it starts with a little research and then an interview. Other times, it involves going on some outdoor trek to gain the experience and capture photos. Although I start each article with excitement, delving deeper often reveals a different reality than I imagined. Some turn out to feel like a grind as I try to shape the subject into a story that hopefully someone will read. Other times, as I go through the initial processes, the story begins to write itself in my mind. In those cases, when I sit down at my computer, I feel like I enter a state of flow as the story appears on the screen.

My first published article was about our friend's coffee shop. I then wrote an article about one of my favorite kids I had ever coached who was heading off to run cross country in college. Since gaining momentum, I have been able to write about adventures I've had with friends and family, multiple paddleboarding excursions, and some of my favorite yard games. I have illuminated the lives of young athletes and written about my friend who makes knives. I told the story of one friend's commercial crabbing business and another friend starting a new coaching gig. I highlighted a friend's children's book and another who lives in a van.

All these stories had meaning from the start for me, and getting to share them gave my writing purpose. I feel very fortunate to have had the opportunity to write about these things I cared about, and I am thankful for the publications that not only gave me a platform but actually paid me to do so. I'm still surprised every time someone says yes to a pitch.

What I didn't understand initially, and which was not as obvious, was the meaning my writing would bring to my own life. In addition to writing stories I expected to connect with, I found significance in articles with which I had no prior relationship. I learned about honeybees and now have hives at my house. I wrote about an artist who then painted a piece for Lindsey's birthday. I have written about a farm on Lindsey's family's original homestead and ended up coaching gymnastics because of an article I wrote about a gymnastics team. I have learned about a mountain biking business and track stars, literal trailblazers, and other contractors. I even wrote about the very place where I learned to play tennis.

The knowledge I have gained and the people I have met have infused my writing with meaning. I value having a purpose when I do something, and my purpose in writing these articles has become the journey of preparing to put the words down. It encompasses the interviews, the notes, the research, and the adventures. It all adds up to sharing the cool stuff people are doing and the awesome places people can visit.

I have been so fortunate in a relatively short period to have told so many stories. Even though the number is ticking up, every time I write about someone else, I'm always nervous about what they will think. It feels like a significant responsibility to be the one telling their story, and my words will be how those who don't know them will perceive them and their actions.

I feel fortunate that I stumbled into this world that has naturally found meaning. I encourage you to pursue endeavors that will give your actions meaning. Most of the articles I referenced, and many more, can be found through links on my website, www.tonymoceri.com. I hope you enjoy reading these stories as much as I enjoyed writing them.

*The meaning of life is to find your gift.
The purpose of life is to give it away.*

*Jump, and you will find out how to
unfold your wings as you fall.*

05

BACK TO WESTERN

Recently, I returned to Western Washington University, my alma mater. Despite being just up the hill from my office, I rarely visit its brick-laid campus where I once spent so much time. I have returned a few times for sporting events, but other than that, I haven't found many reasons to go back. Knowing I would be visiting again brought back nearly twenty years of memories from my daily campus visits. Memories of walking through the Pacific Northwest seasons to class came flooding back. Early fall and late spring classes resulted in slow walks through the warm air, as I tried to avoid sweating before class. On rainy winter days, I would dash from my car, hoping to catch as few raindrops as possible. The best days were always those in fall, with a warm southern breeze gently shaking golden leaves from the branches.

I returned to speak to an environmental journalism class, a visit prompted by my friend Derek Moscato, the professor. He had seen some of the articles I shared on LinkedIn. I was flattered when he originally complimented my work and blown away when he invited me to speak. In college, I took exactly one journalism class, and it went okay at best. My professor told me my style was too embellished for journalism, suggesting

I try creative writing instead. I took them up on that advice by taking exactly one creative writing class. Although I didn't impress that professor either, my lifelong struggles with reading and writing made the invitation to speak to college writers something the younger me would never have believed.

Excited to be on Western's campus again, I arrived early and parked in the southernmost lot to walk the entire campus. I first stopped by the rec center where I had spent so much time playing basketball. With thousands of bricks beneath my feet, I next passed a building added since I graduated and walked up the steps by the environmental science building where I was scheduled to talk. As I strolled by, memories of reading "East of Eden" in the back of my physics class there came flooding back. The adjacent building was where I took biology. As I meandered past Western's many sculptures, familiar buildings surfaced, reviving a rush of memories from all the classes I took. Entering Red Square, the campus's epicenter, I absorbed the vast sea of red bricks around the fountain, a popular student gathering spot on sunny days. I gazed at Bond Hall, where I took numerous history classes for my major. Finally, I climbed the steps of Old Main, reflecting on the concrete steps leading to the brick building before meeting Derek.

After Derek introduced me to the class, I shared my experiences and then fielded questions, feeling somewhat underqualified. Despite having been a writer for four years, it still seems surreal, like something that could end at any moment. The realization hit hard as I spoke about my journey and answered their probing questions about my process—a process I hadn't recognized until then. They inquired about outlines and how stories coalesce, helping me realize that a significant part of my process involves letting the subject simmer. After interviews or experiences, I need time to let the story form in my mind. By the time I sit down to write, the ideas and sometimes entire lines have already replayed in my mind countless times.

In conclusion, my message to the students was straightforward: just go for it. I have no doubt that they each can write great articles. The challenge isn't the writing itself but the courage to expose themselves to potential rejection or unpublished work. I shared stories of my own rejections to emphasize that it's part of the process. To those students and anyone thinking of venturing into writing, I say: take the risk. Not doing so is a far greater one.

As I left the classroom and descended the concrete steps, walking once more on the red bricks, I felt inspired by the students' potential and rejuvenated to continue my own writing journey. As I returned to my truck, I savored the nostalgic feeling of a school day without any homework.

> *It is the sweet, simple things of life which are the real ones after all.*

> *Every pizza is a personal pizza if you try hard and believe in yourself.*

06

COLD PIZZA

Cold pizza is surprisingly good. I hadn't had it in a long time because Harper always calls dibs on the leftovers. While the taste remains good, owing to the unchanged ingredients, the unexpectedly pleasant texture is what really stands out. The cheese becomes slightly dense, giving way to the marinara sauce, which can be a bit granular but still tasty. The crust, always crucial, maintains its integrity even when cold, becoming a bit dryer but not unpleasantly so. Toppings vary in how well they endure the cold; pepperoni and pineapple tend to fare the best. However, surprisingly, the cold sausage on a pizza is remarkably satisfying.

This was some leftover Cowboy Pizza from Papa Murphy's. She pulled out the box; yes, I know Papa Murphy's doesn't typically use boxes, but after leaving a friend's house, we ended up with a few slices in a donut box. That's a good reminder—donuts are really good too, especially an old-fashioned dipped in coffee. There are few things more enjoyable than sitting in a little donut shop with orange booths from the '70s, dipping a glazed old-fashioned donut into some mediocre coffee.

Anyway, Harper isn't fond of the cowboy pizza. Some toppings, specifically the mushrooms, she only tolerates when warm but dislikes when cold. Her favorite pizza is pepperoni, pineapple, and black olive with an olive oil garlic sauce. It's a delightful combination, but I prefer just pineapple or black olives, not both. I watched her eat one piece and then walk away, so I swooped in and finished it off.

It was a good reminder not to deprive ourselves of the little joys in life. These small pleasures truly enhance our experiences. The smells and tastes of simple things can often be overlooked, but they are what make life enjoyable. It's also a good reminder that cold pizza is delicious!

By failing to prepare you are preparing to fail.

Don't mistake activity for productivity.

07

LOST

Life can be a confusing place,

Especially when you start to race.

Take the time, create a map, To prevent that extra lap.

Being lost is part of life,

But why not plan and save some strife?

If on your course you set a mark,

Towards the lighthouse you may embark.

Through the fog that life can bring,

You may hear the sirens sing.

You must ignore their enticing song,

Keep on going, you are strong.

No longer lost, you will see.

How successful you can be.

> *The more that you read, the more things you will know. The more that you learn, the more places you'll go.*

> *Have an adventure. Make memories. Do what you love. Learn something new. Have fun make it special. Live life to the fullest.*

08

DEXTEROUS AND DEFT

Dr. Seuss writes dexterous and deft,

In order for you to pass life's test.

Being nimble, he would say,

Helps live life a better way.

One fish, two fish, red fish, blue fish,

Don't worry about looking foolish.

Keep on trying, just like Knox,

When he learned to rhyme from Fox.

Inspired by little Cindy Lou Who,

If the Grinch can change, so can you.

So, if one day you meet a Wocket,

You will understand Seuss, the prophet.

Taking knowledge from his rhyme,

You will make your life sublime.

Life isn't about finding yourself. Life is about creating yourself.

The future depends on what we do in the present.

09

DESIGNING LIFE

I believe that the decisions we make and the actions we take, for the most part, determine what happens to us in life. Yes, things happen that are out of our control, but usually, we get to decide. The way I like to put it is, "Happen to life, don't let life happen to you." My point is that I constantly hear people saying that something happened to them, and that is now their excuse for why something didn't go the way they wanted or planned. If, instead of sitting around waiting for things to happen, we are proactive in making what we want to occur, then we start to take control. From my experience, doing this has a snowball effect.

What begins as one choice can have a compounding effect, leading to dictating the way your life will go. If we don't proactively decide to take our life where we want, outside influences will do it for us. But, if we say, "This is what I want to do, and this is where I want to go," and take action to make those desires a reality, then they will become just that. There are all sorts of methods out there for making the life you want a reality. Some people use vision boards; others are very goal-centric, setting specific markers to hit along their path. My approach has been to understand what I want out of life, which often changes, and design a world that provides those wants.

The most important thing for me is to have the freedom and flexibility to do what I want, when I want. To go along with that, I want to have the financial means and physical ability to jump on those opportunities when they arise. The majority of these things are simple, like being able to take my daughter to school and still hang on the basketball court as I age. I want to have the option to impulsively take a hike with my friend or go on vacation with my family. I like jumping on a new business idea or a good real estate deal at a moment's notice, just as much as taking a day to putter around my property, listening to podcasts and audiobooks. I want to be able to coach youth sports in the middle of the day and say yes to freelance writing gigs. I like buying a ridiculous amount of yard games and driving them around in my 1985 VW Westfalia in hopes that I bump into someone to play them with.

I am happy to say that, for the most part, I have designed this life, and it works well for me. It didn't happen overnight, and it took me a long time to understand what I wanted to design. It also changes along with my life situation and age. My design is not right for everyone, heck, it probably isn't right for anyone else, and yours probably won't be either. But that's what makes it your design. It isn't some life you see people portraying on social media or what your parent, spouse, child, friend, teacher, or coach wants for you. It's what you want. Now all those people, and many more, will have an impact and likely some good advice, but it isn't their life you are living.

So, be proactive, design a life you want to live and make decisions that move you in that direction. If you happen to life instead of letting life happen to you, those visions of what you have in your mind will be much more likely to occur. I don't have a magic bullet for making this happen, but hopefully, in these pages, you will find some tools to help you live a life of your own design. Whether you are looking for the freedom to spend more time with your family, the means to buy a new home, or the physical ability to climb a mountain, it's all within reach. Often when we think of some goal that is so big, it makes even getting started overwhelming. So instead of focusing on just the end goal, focus on little steps that can be integrated into your life that will move you in the right direction. It is important to remember that while there are these places we want to get in life, we still need to enjoy living in the present.

It took me a while to understand that life truly was a journey, not a destination, as I pushed towards some financial goals that I thought would complete my life design. Instead, I came to understand that what I needed to do was design a life that I enjoyed living right now and that I could do that and still keep working toward future goals. My method for living a life I enjoy now, while always trying to improve, is the 1% infinity approach. In the coming pages, you will find a piece on the 1% infinity approach.

What I have found is living in a way that allows me to enjoy living in the now, and building towards the future, I feel like a weight has been lifted off my shoulders. I don't have to reach some mark tomorrow but feel good that I'm moving in that direction. At the same time, while enjoying living my life every day, not only am I happy in the moment, but I can also look back fondly on the life that has been lived.

It's your life, design it the way you want. You are the only one who can make it happen; no one will do it for you. If they do, you can bet it won't be your design. The exciting part is all you have to do is dream it up and proactively start building that design. The other exciting part is you can change on the fly. If the idea of the design was better than the reality, then rearrange and keep moving forward.

Do not go where the path may lead, go instead where there is no path and leave a trail.

Be like a duck. Remain calm on the surface and paddle like hell underneath.

10

SITTING DUCK

Life is not a game of chance;

you make a move, and that's your stance.

Just like in chess, you create your luck;

without a plan, you're a sitting duck.

Under the water, your legs must flutter;

and your mind must be cleared of clutter.

While living this way may feel like a chore,

this approach is will let you soar.

Continuous improvement is better than delayed perfection.

The road to success is always under construction.

1% INFINITY

The principle of one percent infinity posits that focusing on improving by just one percent at a time leads to incremental and substantial long-term benefits. While not a new concept and with unclear origins, this strategy is applicable across all life's aspects.

Let's consider a financial example with clearly defined numbers. Imagine your goal is to pay off a $300,000 home loan in 15 years instead of 30. You might plan to save money and make one large payment at the year's end. Although well-intentioned, saving a large sum for a specific purpose often proves more difficult than anticipated. Instead, by applying the 1% infinity approach and slightly increasing your monthly mortgage payment, you gradually reduce your loan's amortization schedule without it feeling burdensome.

Attempting to achieve fitness all at once often proves to be an overwhelming and unachievable task. However, making small, manageable changes, such as incorporating more vegetables into your diet or walking daily, can lead to sustainable health improvements. When it takes an extreme diet or being at the gym at 6:00 am, it is easy to make excuses and never start or quickly quit. However, if we do it little by little, it is easier to start and continue doing it. Each day just try making your health 1% better. It might be eating more vegetables, going for a walk, or taking a yoga class. Maybe you skip dessert on Saturday or have water instead of soda with dinner. One significant change I made was to stop buying ice cream. It sounds like no big deal, and for many people, it isn't, but I'm eating it if it is in the house. I find that if I simply don't buy it, the temptation isn't there, and I don't miss it... well, that much.

For entrepreneurs, this can be a great way to continuously improve your business without becoming totally consumed by it. It is easy when you have your own business to get lost in your work and never step away. There is always more to do, but what are you sacrificing? By following the 1% infinity approach, you have the reassurance that you are continuously improving your business but without it dominating every bit of your time.

With the wide range of things I have going on, I try to pick one thing every day that may get overlooked on a busy day that will make things 1% better. This can be simple, like learning something new, getting in some extra exercise, organizing my office, or reaching out to a potential business partner.

Whatever area you want to improve, give the 1% infinity a try. As you try this, the 1% is the easy part. Tomorrow you might wake up and grab a piece of fruit for breakfast as your 1%. The hard part is the infinity, but that is the key to making these small steps lead to big improvements. Good luck, and send me a message letting me know what your 1% is for tomorrow.

> *"If it's true that time is money, don't you think the real question is how you should spend it?"*

> *"Carpe Diem"*

12

GET UP

Every day, to improve.

I wake up early and get on the move.

I move my body for my health,

Get my work done to grow my wealth.

Checking boxes all day long.

Gives me family time later on.

Seize the day I will do.

I hope that you will too!

Yesterday is gone. Tomorrow has not yet come. We have only today. Let us Begin.

Know thy self, know thy enemy. A thousand battles, a thousand Victories.

GET BETTER

Getting better every day,

makes life grand, I have to say.

Improve yourself, as you can,

I promise you, you'll become a fan.

Read a book, or take a walk,

make yourself more than all talk.

Lift some weights, complete your work,

you will find it comes with perks.

Advance yourself when you wake,

a fantastic person you shall make.

> "Life is like riding a bicycle. To keep your balance, you must keep moving."

> "There's no such thing as work-life balance. There are work-life choices, and you make them, and they have consequences."

14

BALANCE

The pursuit of extreme success is currently in vogue. Authors and podcast hosts often champion the notion of achieving maximum potential through intense focus. By excelling in one specific area, you aim to achieve greatness. Professional athletes and billionaires, known for their extreme focus, are often cited as examples who have achieved outstanding success and reached their industry's pinnacle.

Don't misunderstand me; I too consume this information. It's invaluable, and we can all learn from it. However, if this doesn't resonate with you, you're in good company with the majority of the population. It's not that you lack a desire for success; rather, you don't focus solely on one aspect of life.

Many people do not have a single focus in life. Most of us are not wired that way. I know I'm not. I will be lucky to focus long enough to finish this section of the book right now. This does not mean you cannot live a successful life or have outstanding achievements, but it means they are probably defined differently than society's current definition. They may not make the news, and they might not result in a gold medal or public accolades, but they will have real meaning in your life. They will allow you to live the life you want to live and impact those that are important to you. You will define a successful life and use the tools in this book to live that life. You get to decide what that looks like. You may want to get a job and work in it for thirty years; you might want to have a new job every year, or you might not want a job at all. Whether it is travel, family, money, recreation, leisure, work, charity, pets, health, or all the above, you get to decide.

What this means is that you can create a life that allows you to wake up every day and get to do the things you love to do. It is not that you won't have to do things you don't want to do, but the idea is to design a life in which you have the time, money, knowledge, and physical ability to do what you decide is most important. Achieving a life of balance is not necessarily easy or without some sacrifice. There is a reason so many people feel their life is out of balance, and some think that achieving that balance is impossible. It is hard to achieve balance, and just as hard to stay there.

As your priorities in life change, you will become out of balance. Significant life events, planned or unplanned, can easily knock you off kilter. We know there will be wobbles or times when you get knocked totally off balance, but once you have the tools, you can always regain that balance. What we want is to create a world that, by design, is balanced. That means we must build an environment conducive to this balance and form habits that support that world. These habits will be in all areas of life, ranging from health and fitness to saving and investing. It's more meaningful time with family and the ability to explore the world. It's leisure time and accomplishing big goals. You will not be creating habits for the sake of creating habits. You will be creating habits that will bring consistency to your life. It will not happen overnight, but by creating the correct habits and building on them, the life you are seeking will come to fruition. I want to point out that these habits are not going to be drastic changes that throw your life into chaos. It will be baby steps that, one by one, will slowly progress and eventually become very impactful.

Remember, the goal here is not to go from one extreme to another but to create balance. We do not want to be a pendulum or a roller-coaster but a steady ship or train. We want a constant trajectory where we can enjoy the ride. Your ship may be headed towards a huge bank account or rock-hard abs. You might be headed towards the garden you always dreamed of or a good book on a sandy beach. The important piece is that whatever it is, that one thing is not your sole focus. There are so many other pieces of your life that are important. You don't want to be on that pendulum and swing away from some important pieces while diving headfirst into something. You will be on a trajectory to reach your goals but do so in a balanced way. It will not be at the expense of other essential areas of your life but in harmony with them. With a methodical approach, you will build this balanced life in the way you want it to be done. There is no one correct answer, just your answer. Remember that answer will change and evolve as your age and life circumstances change. The great thing is you will be positioned in a way that when circumstances change, it will not be a free fall but will be little curves in the tracks in order to stay balanced.

Living a life of balance will take directed effort to make happen but the payoff should be not just a balanced life but also a balanced mind. The stress of getting everything done or the stress of missing out on important moments should wane as your world allows for both the capacity and time to involve a wider range of life experiences. The mental space a balanced life creates is just as important as the tangible pieces that you can see and touch.

In a world that gets faster paced every day staying in balance can feel challenging, and that's ok. There is often a feeling that without specialization or intense focus you will be left behind. That feeling is normal but shouldn't be overpowering. If there is one thing that our rapidly changing world should prove, it's that we don't know what's coming next. Having a balanced life that allows us to adapt to the unknown changes does prepare us for the future. It will let us have the time to learn about the newest technology or the ability to pivot should our profession become obsolete. We will have the time and connection with our kids to help them grow in a world we never envisioned. It means that when the next great opportunity arises, we have the capacity to capitalize on that opportunity. It allows us to not just slog through life but have fun and enjoy the wonderful things going on around us.

Living a life of balance isn't a magic trick, it's proactively living to make that balance happen. To achieve this balance, whatever it looks like for you, it's taking the time and effort to work on the pieces that need to improve. This may be taking the time to cook meals at home and spend more time with your family. It could start by canceling some subscriptions to improve your financial situation. It might mean taking the stairs instead of the elevator to burn a few more calories. It might mean spending less time at the gym and more time learning a new skill.

Whichever way your life is out of balance take steps to start swinging the pendulum the other direction. If you are the type of person that may swing too far, that's fine; you can always swing back. It's step by step and piece by piece that you create a life of balance and keep it there. It will take constant maintenance but once in balance, you will be more aware and have an easier time making those tweaks when necessary. It all starts with one action leading to some new habits so pick one thing and start getting in balance.

> *Don't get so busy making a living that you forget to make a life.*

> *I don't think any man is contented when there are things left undone.*

15

WORKING IN BURSTS

Today, I went for a walk with a friend to discuss potential professional collaboration. We originally met through Moceri Construction, where he first became a customer. We're close in age, our children are similar ages, and we live nearby, which has naturally fostered a bond. Initially, he was about to retire from the Coast Guard, and during his construction project, we talked about potentially working together afterwards, as he was interested in entering the construction sector.

It's been a few years, and after trying out employment with others, he has decided to start his own business, so the timing was right to reconnect. During our three-mile walk, we talked about the construction industry, bookkeeping, real estate, coaching youth, family time, and a few other topics. Our conversation, initially meant to focus on potential construction collaborations, naturally meandered through various subjects.

After the walk, I reflected with Lindsey that despite knowing him for years, he might not fully grasp our lifestyle. The standard nine-to-five schedule has never suited us, not because we dislike working, but rather because we thrive on a flexible schedule that includes completing intense projects that often require long hours. We frequently manage multiple projects that, although unrelated, tend to have overlapping deadlines or similar timing needs. Lindsey might have weeks where she works every day, followed by periods with more sporadic tasks. My routine is similar, and as I write this, I realize I'm crafting this book in the same way—some days I write extensively, followed by periods where I don't write at all.

We've realized that what works for us is working in bursts. This might seem unusual to many, but it's effective for our dynamic lifestyle. It's akin to the 'work hard, play hard' mentality, though our rest periods are often more about quiet reflection than active leisure. Sometimes, the work bursts are followed by calm periods, reminiscent of letting a field lie fallow after a productive season.

While this approach may not suit everyone, I appreciate the rhythm of working in bursts. It keeps our work life vibrant and maintains efficiency. Each work session is highly focused and timed to when we're most motivated. Whether it's impromptu article writing, evaluating potential real estate investments, or managing our custom home projects at Moceri Construction, we engage only in tasks that genuinely fit and feel right.

In essence, working in bursts suits our personality and lifestyle, and while it might not be for everyone, it's worth considering if traditional routines feel constraining. As I wrap up this burst of writing, I'm ready to switch gears to the next task.

Time is really the only capital that any human being has and the thing that they can least afford to waste or lose.

True enjoyment comes from activity of the mind and exercise of the body; the two are ever united.

16

THE WALKING MEETING

Meetings consume much of our time, playing a crucial role in business operations and decision-making. Inevitably, we find ourselves in conference rooms and coffee shops, tackling problems, making decisions, or just connecting with others. I was poised for a standard meeting in a coffee shop when someone suggested a walk instead. I loved the idea and have since been scheduling walking meetings whenever possible.

Recent studies equate sitting with the new smoking. Most of us don't move nearly enough. It isn't that people desire to sit all day; their professions often necessitate it. Although standing desks and treadmill desks offer partial solutions, they do not address the fundamental need to simply get out and move.

Walking meetings offer a valuable opportunity to exercise and breath fresh air. I feel more energized and creative as we walk and talk. Unexpected sights during these walks can spark new thoughts or offer fresh perspectives, combining the benefits of a 30-minute walk with creative breakthroughs discussed in this book.

Next time you schedule a meeting, if you're not poring over documents and mobility is feasible, consider a walking meeting.

We were on a break!

Me thinks that the moment my legs begin to move my thoughts begin to flow.

17

THE 30-MINUTE WALK

A few years back, Lindsey and I attended a Peak Performance class taught by Dr. Ralph Vernacchia, a sports psychologist at Western Washington University. Dr. Vernacchia, with his experience on the U.S. Olympic Team, specialized in helping individuals reach their full potential.

In the class, he shared the benefits of his daily thirty-minute walk used as a tool to stimulate circulation and clear his mind. These breaks, filled with fresh air and exercise, divided his day, enhancing his efficiency and greatly reducing stress. My dad, who told us about the class, has effectively integrated these daily walks into his routine. Honestly, I am still working to make it a habit, but I increasingly find time for it. Each time I manage, it significantly reinforces all the benefits Dr. Vernacchia outlined.

You might be thinking, 'Where can I find thirty minutes in a day?' Initially, I viewed it as lost time. However, seeing it as an opportunity to return more refreshed and efficient changes that perception. Utilizing this time for problem-solving can turn out to be highly productive. If it also relieves stress, then it enhances your performance in all life's aspects. I suggest taking a thirty-minute walk to think this over.

And into the forest I go to lose my mind and find my soul.

Every problem has a solution; it may sometimes just need another perspective.

18

WALK

Taking a walk to have a talk.

Can free the mind, you will see.

With blood now flowing, your mind starts growing.

Ideas evolving and problems resolving.

This time in motion will have been wisely chosen.

When it's next time to talk, why not combine it with a walk?

> *It is health that is real wealth. And not pieces of gold and silver.*

> *To keep the body in good health is a duty... otherwise we shall not be able to keep our mind strong and clear.*

19

FEEL SICK ACT SICK

I often find myself in denial about being sick. It's not that I frequently fall ill, but when I do catch a cold, I tend to attribute the symptoms to allergies—a dubious claim unless I've been snuggling with pets. As the pain in my nasal passages and slight throat soreness settle in, I'm aware of what's ahead yet lie to myself, initially dismissing it as a fleeting anomaly and choosing to ignore it.

The next phase is believing I can preempt the illness. This involves guzzling herbal tea with vitamin C-rich rose hips, popping a cold pill, snacking on an apple, taking a zinc tablet, and then stepping into a sauna. A meal rich in garlic and nettles drizzled with Tabasco Sauce, and a glass of bourbon supposedly seals the deal.

Despite these efforts, I don't disparage them since they do provide temporary relief. However, conquering the ailment entirely without succumbing to it proves elusive. Now, writing from bed after several days of denial and exhausting all remedies, I acknowledge my actual state. No severe symptoms—just a persistent runny nose that leans me towards an allergy misdiagnosis. Yet, after days of this routine, I doubt it's just allergies.

Reluctant to let this drag on, I've embraced sound advice I once received: if you feel sick, act sick. Embracing this, I am now resting, reading, writing, and perhaps watching a show or two. Rarely do I relax enough, so maybe this is my body's way of demanding a slowdown. It's hardly catastrophic; something beneficial might even emerge from it. So, embrace the sick, and when you feel ill, let your actions reflect it. Your body will be grateful.

*If you don't know where you are going,
any road will get you there.*

*Roads were made for journeys,
not destinations.*

20

ROAD TRIPPING

Lindsey and I love to travel. Since we first got together, taking trips has been a big part of what we do. We have taken longer trips flying across the country or an ocean. We regularly escape the Pacific Northwest winters by flying to a beach or pool with sunny weather. We also do a lot of road-tripping. These often start from our house with a combination of camping and hotels or vacation rentals, but we have also flown and road-tripped.

We find that mentally we are excited about the destination, but it really is the journey that we love. There is the adventure part of it that you never know what will happen, who you will meet, or what you will find. There are also the unknowns that are known. I know that doesn't make sense, but it does. It's the pieces that put together any great adventure that we know will be a part of it, but we must wait to have the details revealed.

It's beautiful scenery and changing weather. It's dirty gas stations and unexpected traffic. It's little cafes with great food and panic eating of gut-bomb fast food. It's walking small towns, learning their history, buying trinkets, and meeting the locals. It's hiking to incredible viewpoints, empty casts with the fly rod, and pans of rocks with no glimmer of gold.

All these pieces and so many more are what makes the journey so grand. These are the things that are missed when flying. The little details are skipped, and while flying to get poolside is nice, and certainly, on my schedule, it is often less nourishing than a road trip. The journey is the meat of the sandwich, a sandwich with really good bread. The bread is so good that you would be happy to eat it on its own. You have a slice here and a slice there and enjoy every bite, but when you add the layers, each bite becomes an adventure in your mouth. The journey is those layers. It's the mayo and mustard, the provolone and salami, and that crisp piece of lettuce. The point of all this is to enjoy the journey because that's what most of life is, and frankly, it's often the best parts. Destinations can be a letdown with unrealistic expectations. The journey is what it is. Filled with unexpected twists and turns, it's exciting, sometimes painful, and fun!

I am far from the first person to say it, and I'm sure I won't be the last, but make sure to enjoy the journey. This might be a day trip, a weekend getaway, or a summer-long road trip. It might just be the road trip of life. Whatever it is, enjoy all the little pieces. They make up most of life, so give the journey credit and enjoy what it brings.

As I write this, I'm sitting next to a roaring river while Lindsey and Harper sleep in the camper. I experienced a passing shower, not enough to ruin the paper, which was unexpected as it was 90 degrees and sunny yesterday.

This piece of writing was Lindsey's idea as we traveled to our destination. We were heading to our favorite camping spot, and while we were eager to get here, we reveled in how much we enjoyed the journey. It involved road work and making sandwiches in a parking lot. Getting ice and batteries at a gas station and a beautiful drive down familiar roads.

Even though this was not a new destination we were heading to, the journey was unique, and always is. We stopped by the North Cascades National Park ranger station, which we had never done before. We had driven by dozens of times but were so focused on the destination we never bothered to pull in or really even knew it was there. It turns out it's one of the best we have been to. It has a little museum and friendly rangers giving information about hiking trails. We then stopped in a little town to get candy and inspiration. Familiar shops flanked by new ones always get us excited about what local entrepreneurs are doing. We note ideas that we may want to seam into something someday and always check out the local real estate. We stimulate the economy by purchasing things we don't need, then head off on our journey. I love being at our destination, it is one of my happy places, but I'm already excited for the journey home. There will be new things to see and experiences to be had. Music to sing to and games to played while we take in the scene. One of my most significant memories of this trip will be just how green everything is and how high the water is. Although I could do without the drips, I'm once again experiencing smudging my ink. The burnt trees are a reminder of just how badly we need this rain.

Well, I'm not sure what this weather is going to do, so I'm going to start a campfire so that Lindsey and Harper have some warmth when they venture out. I'm also going to throw some bacon in a pan on the fire, which is a big motivator. But really, it is the journey of making the fire that will be the best part, just like the rest of the trip.

Life is such a great teacher, but I'm such a slow learner.

Life is about taking chances trying new things, having fun, making mistakes, and learning.

21

VAN LESSONS

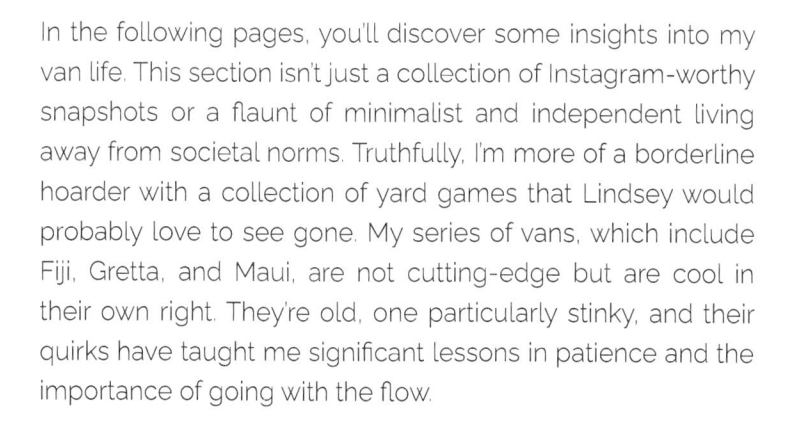

In the following pages, you'll discover some insights into my van life. This section isn't just a collection of Instagram-worthy snapshots or a flaunt of minimalist and independent living away from societal norms. Truthfully, I'm more of a borderline hoarder with a collection of yard games that Lindsey would probably love to see gone. My series of vans, which include Fiji, Gretta, and Maui, are not cutting-edge but are cool in their own right. They're old, one particularly stinky, and their quirks have taught me significant lessons in patience and the importance of going with the flow.

Our first van, which we still own, is Fiji, and the stories of Gretta and Maui will be revealed shortly. Each van has its tale and character, encapsulating various aspects of our lives and travels.

The first narrative, "Top Speed," was initially crafted for a travel website that my wife and I run. While intended to be humorous and to share one of our favorite travel spots, compiling this narrative led me to reflect on some unintended yet valuable life lessons.

The first lesson is about the importance of slowing down—taking the time to enjoy the surroundings, absorb the beauty around us, and truly live in the moment. Admittedly, I've struggled with pacing my life, often rushing from one moment to the next, so remembering to slow down is crucial.

The second lesson revolves around not worrying too much about others' opinions. Living life to the rhythm of your own drum, or in my case, the hum of an old VW engine, should be liberating. Sure, you'll meet folks who might not appreciate your lifestyle or choices, but it's important to surround yourself with people who respect your individuality.

Following these initial reflections are stories about how Fiji came into our lives, and subsequently, the narratives of Gretta and Maui. The concluding part is a reflective piece I wrote a few years ago, which helped me realize just how much these vans have taught me about life.

*Still round the corner, there may wait
a new road or a secret gate.*

*If everything seems under control,
you're just not going fast enough.*

22

TOP SPEED

Taking a little time away from reality is one of the best parts of travel. When you enter a VW Westfalia, you are instantly transported to a different time. This time, I was told once by a mechanic, is Vanagon Time. We were getting a pre-purchase inspection on a 1985 VW Vanagon, and this friendly VW expert was trying to implore to me that these campers are more than just cabinets and a cool pop-top. I didn't really know what he meant because not only do I know very little about cars, at the time, I knew nothing about Vanagon's. Vanagon's are known for breaking down, overheating, and being totally gutless. During the test drives around town, I didn't really notice that her top speed was a little slower than most and, even worse going uphill.

Once we bought her and drove around a bit, I started to understand what the mechanic meant about Vanagon time due to the lack of speed, but, as someone who is pretty wound up, I decided that a bit slower pace was probably good for me.

Flash forward to our first real road trip in our newly purchased van. We were heading over Hwy 20 towards Mazama, WA, and the reality of how many horses I was dealing with became very clear. If you have not driven the North Cascades Highway, it is a beautiful drive. Heading from west to east you begin with the Skagit River on the passenger side of the van. This medium-size river has a fast-paced current with its ripples shimmering in the summer sun. The Skagit is home to elk, eagles and people fishing. All of which may be spotted on your drive. Little towns dot the North Cascade highway as you meander your way upstream. In these small towns businesses come and go as there is seasonality to Highway 20 as the pass closes in the winter due to the large amount of snowfall and risk of avalanches. In these small towns, you will find little bakeries and classic diners. Little gas stations can fill both your van and your belly or if you time it right you may find a roadside stand selling Washington State cherries, one of our state's best treats.

As you leave the little towns behind and enter the North Cascades National Park you will not be greeted by large old lodges as you will in other national parks but will be met by the tranquil beauty of the natural environment. You also may be welcomed by a long line of traffic as RV's and old vans slowly make their way through the park. As you grip your steering wheel in frustration take a breath and enjoy the scene around you. Driving through the park is an immersive wilderness experience as good as any Planet Earth episode you may see. Birds will be abundant, a deer is likely and if you get lucky you might spot a black bear which we have seen in the park on multiple occasions. The most exciting spotting for us was seeing a wolverine cross the road in front of us.

As the winding road takes you through forest tunnels you will get the feeling that Bigfoot may jump out in front of you. I have yet to spot one but am still holding out hope. As you reach the Gorge overlook trail you get an idea of the grandeur that the park is preparing to reveal. The large waterfall on the left leads steeply down to Gorge Lake created by a dam on the Skagit River. This is the first of three lakes all created by dams.

The next two are Diablo and Ross Lakes. Both offer their own forms of beauty and opportunity for recreation and camping. While this trip was all about getting our van through the park, there is no lack of splendor to be seen within its boundaries. Diablo is smaller but the highway takes you right across it giving you an up-close view of the pristine lake. Ross Lake, unless a detour is taken, is viewed from above. It's the largest of the three lakes and the deep blue color makes it seem a piece of fiction. This climb up from the lakes is where the scale of the park begins to be seen as the peaks of the cascades stop hiding behind trees. This is also where the struggles begin for an '85 Westfalia.

The road is steep and, most of the time, two lanes with the occasional passing lane. On previous trips over the pass, I would get road rage being stuck behind a line of RVs. I quickly discovered that would not be an issue on this trip. Not only could I not keep up with RVs, I was now the one holding up traffic. With the pedal to the metal, we were heading over the Cascades at a blazing 35mph! As the lineup formed behind us, our anxiety began to build. I was frustrated that I was now the problem, and Lindsey's anxiety was going through the roof. Harper was little at the time so too young to let us know that she was probably getting car sick. Lindsey suggested we pull over to let the line of traffic go by which was probably the correct thing to do but I was worried that if we pulled over, we would never get moving uphill again. The thought of losing what little momentum we had was too much for me to handle so I pushed on. Eventually, we made it to a passing lane and the cars zipped past. Some friendly enough to give us a one-finger wave.

We trudged along, slowly but surely making our way to our destination. As we took in the high mountain peaks and cascading waterfalls I had a moment of my own kind of excitement. In the distance, I could see a vehicle we were actually gaining on. As we approached a passing lane appeared, and I went for it. I would now be the one doing the passing. As I bragged to Lindsey about the accomplishment it was slightly diminished as the vehicle revealed itself to be a '60s VW Van. As we passed, we excitedly waved to each other as is common practice in the VW Van world. I have tried to get this tradition going in other vehicles with little to no success.

With my ego beginning to grow, Fiji was quick to put me back in check. As we climbed toward Rainy Pass, I'll give you one guess how it got its name, our home on wheels began to heat up. As Fiji worked to get over the pass her temperature gauge climbed. Getting past halfway we started to get worried. Seeing the red light of death come on would mean us sitting on the side of the road waiting for her to cool off while I steamed in frustration. To stave off an overheating situation, we went into action. On this hot summer day, we cranked the heat and turned the fan on full blast to get some heat out of her system. Upon doing this it was clear that it was our first time running the fan because in addition to a blast of unwelcome heat we were greeted by years of mouse bedding. As Lindsey screamed that she had to turn it off, I screamed that we couldn't or we would overheat. With bits of newspaper and foam fluttering in the air, we one wheel turn at a time made it to the top of the pass.

Relieved to have made it to the top we were now rolling downhill at a respectable speed with the windows down and the heat off. Our stress levels dropped, and we were soon once again enjoying the van life. I am happy to report that we did eventually make it to our destination. We ended up having a great camping trip in the pop top. I highly recommend a journey through the Cascades and, if possible, in a vehicle that forces you to take in the scenery at a slower pace.

> *Nearly all the best things that came to me in life have been unexpected, unplanned by me.*

> *Life is a succession of lessons which must be lived to be understood.*

23

NAMING FIJI

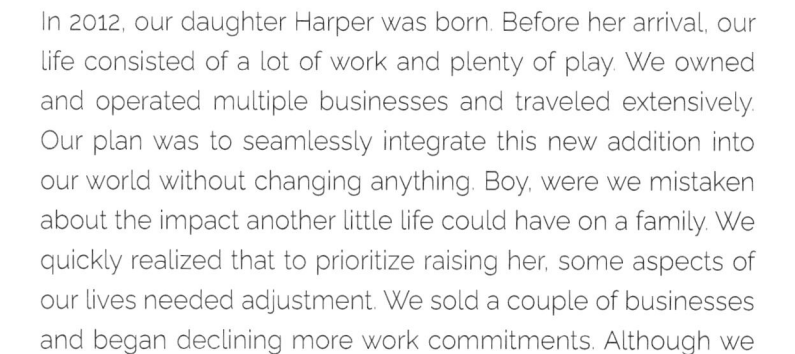

In 2012, our daughter Harper was born. Before her arrival, our life consisted of a lot of work and plenty of play. We owned and operated multiple businesses and traveled extensively. Our plan was to seamlessly integrate this new addition into our world without changing anything. Boy, were we mistaken about the impact another little life could have on a family. We quickly realized that to prioritize raising her, some aspects of our lives needed adjustment. We sold a couple of businesses and began declining more work commitments. Although we wanted travel to remain a significant part of her life, we soon learned that traveling with a child would be different from what we had imagined. The reality was that what is fun with a child in tow differs from what is fun without.

Initially, I struggled to accept this reality, but Lindsey was adamant that we needed a camper. Her idea was that we would replace some of our flights with road trips. By 2013, I reluctantly came around to the idea and started exploring camping options. Having always camped in tents, we were novices in the camper world, so we looked at everything from teardrop trailers to RVs. Lindsey kept returning to the idea of getting a VW camper van. I was completely against it. The last thing I wanted was to drive around in a hippie van, reminiscent of the early 80s vibes my parents had embraced; that was not me.

We ended up considering the newer VW Vans made in the early 2000s. Not being mechanically inclined, the newer models seemed like a better option than the older ones and felt less like the hippie stereotype to me. We test drove a few and were close to purchasing one when we realized how costly these vans were to maintain. Shifting away from those, Lindsey circled back to the 80s models of the VW Westfalia, specifically those made after 1984 because they are water-cooled instead of air-cooled.

When Lindsey sets her mind on finding something, she finds it. She bombarded me with potential purchases until I capitulated. After she showed me several VW Vanagon's, she finally had one for us to view in Bellingham. At that point, I was still firmly against it. I was anxious about the maintenance, even before seeing the van. However, after exploring its features like the kitchen, pop-top, and cabinets, I was intrigued. It seemed like it could meet our family's needs for road trips. A pre-purchase inspection revealed the van was in good condition, which finally wore down my defenses. We purchased our first Vanagon, a 1985 Westfalia.

I decided to name the van Fiji, hoping to bring a bit of the tropical vibe we were missing into our travels. While our friends flew to actual Fiji—a place I still wish to visit—the van reshaped our lives. Our passion for camping and exploring the outdoors flourished, and the memories we've created with Harper are invaluable. We've explored parts of the Pacific Northwest we likely would never have seen and have enjoyed countless local camping trips.

This old van has not only provided us with endless family adventures but also taught us valuable lessons about flexibility and the unexpected joys of life. Fiji has become a beloved member of our family, symbolizing our adventures and a lifestyle shift from high-flying vacations to grounding road trips. It reminds us that life's best moments often come from the unplanned and the casual detours from our intended paths.

> *Traveling in the company of those we love is home in motion.*

> *This is how memories are made... by going with the flow.*

24

FIJI

Buying a van was never my plan I wanted a beach where I needed a fan.

Jet setting to places in a faraway land, was what I thought would make life feel grand.

Instead what I got were wild adventures, that taught me that life had a wide range of pleasures.

Now when I drive, I am yelling hell yeah, while I rock out in my VW Westfalia.

With a couch and a table, it's my home on four wheels, it even has a kitchen for cooking my meals.

A better design I cannot think of, this old van has become something I love.

Camping with family out in the woods, this Fiji always puts us all in good moods.

While at times her engine runs oh so hot, stranded this vehicle has left us not.

With a few extra cranks and maybe a jump, when that engine starts roaring my heart begins to pump.

I know what's ahead is all sorts of fun, when originally I thought this would take me from sun.

My ideas of life had just been so marred but really I couldn't read the Tarot Card.

There were things in my life I couldn't envision, because I thought I'd move with precision.

Fiji taught me that change is nothing to fear and the outcome you see is not always clear.

A move that I thought was ending the show was really a step in starting my flow.

Whether sending an email on her little brown table or dozing to sleep like a baby in a cradle.

Fiji has taught me to slow my life down, and enjoy those moments when we get out of town.

No longer do I fantasize about tropical places as the morning sun shines on the mountain's westerly faces.

I know now that wherever I am is where I'm supposed to be, because in this little van it's just my family and me.

The memories we make are what life's all about, so when life takes a turn be sure not to pout.

Of life's unexpected twists I am now a fan, all because Lindsey had us buy a van.

Safe Driving is no Accident.

There's a gentility on the road. A direct or personal question is out of bounds. But this is simple good manners anywhere in the world.

25

SELLING GRETTA AND PICKING UP MAUI

Lindsey and I, for a period of time, became very interested in VW Vanagons from the years 1984 to 1991. We were always looking at different ones for sale, thinking that having another one would be great. A big part of it was we wanted to leave Fiji all original, so we thought another one would be a good candidate for an engine swap. This more than likely would have involved putting a Subaru engine in it along with some other popular modifications to make these old vans seem a little less old. In all this looking, and while enjoying Fiji so much, Lindsey decided that she would like to have a Vanagon be her daily driver. Finding a people mover, so no kitchen and no pop-top, would be a good option. Ideally, the bed would still fold down in the back, and it would have rear-facing seats making it a seven-seater.

Sure enough, with enough looking, Lindsey found one she thought would be the perfect candidate. This blue 1986 Vanagon had an impeccable maintenance record and only one previous owner. We were bullish on the Vanagon market and didn't think we could go wrong buying it, so we bought it sight unseen and had it shipped from Sacramento. When the van arrived, it was as clean, in good physical condition, and it ran incredibly well. This new addition to the family would lovingly be named Gretta by Harper, and we were thrilled to have her.

Lindsey drove Gretta as her primary vehicle and was loving life. There is nothing like the puppuppupupup of a Vanagon engine when it is running well, and boy did Gretta purr. The novelty of riding around facing backwards was so fun and something you don't see any more in vehicles. I'm assuming this is a safety concern but we both survived the 80's so figured it would be ok. Her rear seat transformed into a bed which was really nothing more than a novelty since we already had camper van. But who knows, maybe Lindsey was crushing mid-day naps back there. She even had a pop-up table that swung up from the driver's side wall in between the bench and one of the rear facing seats. This was perfect in case a game of cribbage broke out which is known to happen between my friend Casey and me. Gretta quickly became a member of the family, and the throwback vehicle was working as Lindsey's daily driver and I took her for a spin any chance I had.

While Gretta was an incredible van she still was from a different time and the advancement in vehicles had come a long way. The warm summer and early fall days eventually transitioned to wet, cold Pacific Northwest weather. While the old van was holding up, the novelty began to wear off, and a longing for modern conveniences returned. Not needing a van sitting around in our driveway, we already had Fiji in the garage, we decided we would sell Gretta. It was a difficult decision, and a sad day when it happened, but she went to a good home. It actually ended up being a girl who I had graduated high school with who had moved to Orcas Island. The idea of Gretta being an island van sat well with us and we knew she would be well cared for. Not only that, but we also actually made money on the whole transaction which I had never done with a vehicle before.

The sale of Gretta caused two things to happen. One, we now thought we were van experts and that we couldn't go wrong buying them. Two, I got insane seller's remorse. I loved driving Gretta and wanted her back. We felt like we had let a member of the family go and couldn't believe we let a van in such good condition get away. We quickly began the search once more thinking that we could find another great van to enjoy and that maybe we could make some money flipping these things. What a fun way to make money it would be. With our vast knowledge of VW vans, having owned two of them now, and the mechanic ability of a monkey, how could I lose? In my mind, we couldn't.

Desperate to find one, we searched for prospects all over the internet. Sure enough, if you look hard enough, especially with rose-colored glasses, you are sure to find one. We were on vacation in Maui when we found what we were looking for. It was a Blue 1987 VW Vanagon with rear-facing seats. It looked very similar to Gretta, and we assumed it would be just as nice. This van was in San Diego, and instead of having it shipped, I decided I would fly down and get it. For the price of shipping, I could buy my friend and me plane tickets, pay for gas, and get a road trip out of it. This would also allow me to inspect the van on the off chance it wasn't quite what we were thinking.

My friend and I landed in San Diego in the evening, stoked to be on an adventure. I had a cashier's check in my back pocket, and I couldn't wait to get my new van. I did have it in the back of my mind that I wouldn't buy it if it wasn't nice, but I didn't really have a plan for getting us home if that was the case. An Uber driver drove us the thirty minutes from the airport to the seller's home and dropped us off. In looking at the van, and smelling it, it wasn't quite as nice as Gretta had been. Well, it wasn't even close to as nice as Gretta, but it started right up, and with our brief inspection in the dark, it seemed fine. I was still in the mindset that even if I got it home and it wasn't a van we wanted to keep forever, I could still make a little money selling it. In that moment, I had two options. Call another Uber and go rent a car to drive back to Washington, or hand over my check and head up the coast in the van. Obviously, it was an easy decision. So, with the signing of a couple pieces of paper, we were off on a great American road trip.

The first night we were flying high, thrilled to be on an adventure. We cruised up the coast passing through beach towns and taking a picture in front of our friend's old Pita Pit in Hermosa Beach. Wanting to make it a way up the coast, we finally decided some sleep would be in order around midnight. Finding a nice pull-off with a view of the Pacific Ocean, life couldn't have been better. Maui, which was the new vans name because of where we were when we found her, was a people mover like Gretta. As we settled into our spot, we folded down the bench to create our bed, threw our stuff on the rear facing seats and slid into our sleeping bags nestled amongst some car parts the seller had left in the van. With the sound of waves, and the smell of an old van we were just about to drift off into a slumber when some lights shined in the windows. Peeking out it was a couple of sheriffs.

I'm sure they took us for the couple of hippies we looked like and informed us that we were not allowed to camp in this spot and would have to move along. They were cool about it and one of them was into vans. They actually told us to just go find a better hiding place. We ended up pulling into a town and just parking on the side of the road. That is one great thing about these vans, they are pretty incognito campers. At 1:00 in the morning we finally got to sleep. In the morning, we headed for a park at a nearby beach. We used the facilities, and I excitedly ran out onto the beach. This was how life was supposed to be. I was with my lifelong friend Kenny, we were on an adventure, and I had a new van!

The trip north was great as we took in the coastal scene. The speedometer didn't work, but that was a minor issue an app could fix. Maui was treating us well and my love affair was growing. Yes, she was a little rough around the edges and not in pristine condition like Gretta, but I liked that about her. I have a tendency to drive around in well used vehicles. There's less pressure that way. What's one more scratch when scratch and dent is the body style?

We left Southern California as quickly as one can taking the scenic route. We wanted the views but didn't have time in our schedule for many stops but driving the coast in a van is something special and we were having fun. As we got through the beach towns, we decided it was time to stretch our legs and arms by putting our frisbee golf discs to work. We found a course up ahead just past San Luis Obispo and decided to check it out. The course at Heilmann park was great. It was well maintained and had fun holes. Like most courses it can be a little confusing to know exactly where to go from hole to hole and which cage you are throwing to. Lucky for us we got a tour guide. Terry, who may or may not have lived at the park knew the course well and asked if he could play the round with us. We were not ones to say no so our twosome became a threesome and off we went with Terry giving us the scoop on every hole. I can't remember who won which probably means Kenny did, but we had a blast and Terry, and his unique personality will always fondly be remembered.

Back on the road we made the decision to continue up the 101 and to go through San Francisco so that we could drive across the Golden Gate Bridge. As we wound down into the city, we checked the map and saw that there was a traffic jam ahead. My blood pressure shot up and I worried that Maui would overheat like Fiji did. It was a warm day, and I didn't think there was any way we would make it through the stop and go traffic. As we approached Kenny, being a car guy, assured me we would be fine. He had a sense for these things and probably just didn't want me freaking out. In the end Kenny was right and we made it over the Golden Gate Bridge and through the traffic jam without Maui overheating.

As evening was approaching, I was feeling as though I had lucked out with this van. Yes, she had her blemishes, but she was rolling down the road just fine. Just as my chest started to puff out, feeling good about my purchase, we started to notice a little bounce. At first, we chalked it up to a bumpy road, but potholes were nowhere to be seen so unless they were magically appearing under the van, it was the van itself.

We pulled into the town of Ukiah that had a Home Depot and Kenny quickly diagnosed the issue. We had lost a bolt somewhere along the 101. Fortunately, Home Depot had a bolt that would work and with an inexpensive set of wrenches and Kenny's skills we were able to get back on the road within an hour.

While you never want your vehicle to have problems on a road trip, I have to say this stopping point was a little fortuitous. We decided to grab dinner while in town and ended up at Oco Time. Now, I'm a sucker for Asian food and food I've never had before. At this Japanese restaurant they had Okonomiyaki which I would describe as sprout, egg, and noodle pancake. There are a bunch of other ingredients, and it was good. I have been thinking about that meal since the day I left and can't wait to one day return. If you are in the area, check it out.

With full bellies we headed north towards the Redwoods. Kenny had never seen them and while we did get him to these incredible trees unfortunately it was dark. He got to see the size and scale of them, but he will need to return to fully understand the beauty the Redwood forests have to offer. From there we zig zagged our way towards I-5. Detours and closed gas stations had us running on fumes, but we eventually got to the interstate and found some fuel. We slept for a bit at a rest area before heading to Portland to pick up some juniper wood for my brother Dominic. That's a whole other story but the short story is he's a wood nerd. Eager to get home we finished the last four hours of the drive and Maui was finally in Whatcom County.

After dropping Kenny off I made it home dreary eyed but excited to show the van to Lindsey. She took one look at Maui and was not impressed. She hadn't had 1,500 miles to fall in love with the van. To her it was a beat-up old van that now probably stunk worse than when we picked her up. It was clear Maui would be my van and I was ok with that.

Within days of being back in Bellingham the honeymoon was over. The fuel line started leaking gas, and it's a miracle it didn't happen on our road trip. That would obviously be an issue for most cars, but in Vanagon's, fuel leaks are notorious for causing them to burst into flames. Well, that didn't happen, and it was nothing a little money couldn't solve. Back on the road, I was loving driving the van. Lindsey, not so much. Maui had one issue after another. The floor even flooded with coolant and instead of putting carpet back in I laid down a foam alphabet floor my daughter was done with. Even though Maui was hard on my pocketbook, I loved her.

After months of cruising around with my paddleboard on top, sleeping in the back, and having a great summer logic began to prevail. The repair bills were adding up, and once again, having a second van just didn't make sense. Sadly, I listed Maui for sale, thinking I could at least recoup my costs. Breaking even would be a win with all the fun she had provided. Well, that initial listing did not provide any interest. Reluctantly I lowered the price. I then had a few people take a look, but no buyers. I lowered the price once more. Now, more interest but no sale. Finally, I dropped the price to a fire sale level and a couple of sisters who loved vans adopted Maui. It was a sad day, but I was happy she went to a good home, and relieved to shed the constant repair bills.

I learned from this experience that I was not a van expert and that sometimes getting lucky can turn you into a fool. I learned that when you have a good thing, hold onto it. I learned that cutting your losses can be the best move. But most importantly, I learned that going after an adventure is what life is all about. Yes, we wish we still had Gretta, but man, am I glad I got to experience Maui. The experiences and lessons more than offset the cost and aggravation she gave me. Those experiences and lessons are what life's all about.

> *I learn from my mistakes. It's a very painful way to learn, but without pain, the old saying is, there is no gain.*

> *It's good to learn from your mistakes. It's better to learn from other people's mistakes.*

26

LESSONS LEARNED: 1987 VW VANAGON

I'm currently waiting in the back of Maui for Lindsey. Normally, I'd be content here, lounging on the blue cloth seat, feet on the foam alphabet floor, tapping away at my tablet on the pop-out table. I enjoy using the Vanagon as a mobile office. When I do this, I try to park somewhere with a nice view as I operate out of a home office on wheels. I have taken in bay views while I get a little work done between meetings, saving me from driving all the way back to my office. I have often used it as a workspace, aka place to get out of the rain, while Harper is at soccer practice. It's perfect, I can be dry and warm and watch her out there slopping around in the mud. Although it's usually great to use the van this way, today's dreary location and lackluster view leave much to be desired.

I currently have a view out the windshield of a Verizon store and to my right it's stop and go traffic as people try to get home from work. Behind me is a gas station and to my left is a car wash. While old Vanagon's are supposed to be my happy place, unfortunately, they can also be a stress point, leading to elevated blood pressure. This is one of those cases because, in addition to waiting for Lindsey, I am also waiting for AAA to show up and tow my van.

Just as I was exiting the freeway, my van began emitting a terrible buzzing sound, which I've learned signals an oil pressure warning. In addition to the buzzing sound and a flashing red light, I began to smell smoke. I looked in the rearview mirror, because the engine is in the back, and I could see smoke billowing out. I quickly pulled over to assess the situation and found fluid, I think coolant, pouring out, with a belt dangling from the engine. I am no mechanic, but I think it is a bad sign!

Lindsey and the tow truck driver pulled into the parking lot at the same time and looked at me shaking their heads. I would like to think the little bubbles above their heads read "Wow, what a good-looking van, Tony is so lucky he gets to drive that sweet ride." However, I think what they were actually saying was "Why does this moron insist on driving around in this stinky van that clearly needs a total overhaul?"

The tow truck driver was great and got Maui loaded up quickly and off to the mechanic. While I'm sure Lindsey would have rather left me in the parking lot, she was nice enough to give me a ride home. Lindsey accepts my antics and peculiar purchasing habits better than I think anyone else would, but at this point, she began questioning what the long-term plan was with Maui. I deflected and told her about this great writing piece I had been working on while I waited for her.

I could have gotten upset and angry over this situation. It was an obvious inconvenience for Lindsey and me. I would also be spending time and money on the repairs. Instead of getting upset though, I decided I would use it as an opportunity to learn.

- **Lesson #1:**

If you are going to have a junky unreliable vehicle, GET AAA! I have paid for my membership multiple times just with towing. As an added perk, we often get discounts when traveling.

- **Lesson #2:**

If you are not a mechanic, an old vehicle will cost you! I have close to no skills when it comes to working on a car, so any time something goes wrong, I either pay up or get help from some great friends.

- **Lesson #3 –**

I may as well have bought a boat! Boats, from my past experiences, are holes you throw money into. I have historically been good about staying out of those money-draining situations, but as it turns out, old VW Vans are just as bad. I have fallen into the trap once again. I justify it to myself as it is our family toy, but no matter how I frame it, this van is a financial bleeder.

- **Lesson #4:**

Know what you are buying! Buying Maui site unseen was, well, shortsighted.

- **Lesson #5:**

Life is short so enjoy the ride. As illogical, financially stupid, and stressful as this van has been, it is still a blast to drive, a great place to sleep, and a useful office when driving is no longer an option!

The best laid schemes O' mice an' Men often go awry.

There are certain life lessons that you can only learn in the struggle.

27

CAMPING IN THE RAIN

Last year, Leavenworth; this year, Mazama. The meteorologists all predicted rain. Despite numerous checks and a touch of disbelief, the rain was undeniable. Last year, during a thunderstorm in our Honda Element with a pop-top, we barely managed the first night. The storm's onset sent Lindsey, Harper, and myself into cramped quarters too early. After a soggy twelve-hour ordeal, we opted for a hotel as the rain persisted. You'd think I'd learn from such experiences, but perhaps that's giving me too much credit.

It's been about a year, and here I am, writing from our tent as I listen to rain patter on the rainfly. Harper and I, along with my friend Anthony and his two children, are enjoying tent camping. Less than twenty-four hours in, and it's already an adventure. We drove here in my truck, its lumber rack quickly transforming into a makeshift jungle gym upon our arrival. Though our hike along Highway 20 was brief, it amused the kids enough to devour the Doritos before even reaching the campsite. Since then, we've been exploring the surrounding area and gathering around the campfire.

The mothers opted out of this trip, likely relieved to have a quiet house. Though we miss their company, dinner—a Mountain House Meal—amazed Anthony's children, who couldn't believe such tasty food came from a packet. And while I'm not endorsed by Mountain House, I wouldn't mind a sponsorship should any company executives stumble upon this narrative in one of those quaint little free library boxes that grace our neighborhood street corners.

Upon arrival at our campsite, blessed with perfect summer weather, we indulged in gold panning and various yard games. Nestled at the foot of the Cascade Mountains, the landscape, rich with trees yet sparse underbrush, houses a babbling river just steps from our tents, creating a natural ambiance. The day's minor challenge was Anthony coaxing me into an icy river plunge, but he compensated with some fine bourbon by the evening fire. As night fell, I expected another idyllic day, yet the impending rain now casts a shadow of doubt on our plans. The Petz family is likely sleeping peacefully, and Harper is soundly asleep beside me. For now, all I can do is write and wait for dawn.

Rain began at 4:00 AM, disrupting the stillness. I ventured out, hastily securing our campsite against the impending soak. Despite the clear, starry sky at bedtime, which suggested a fleeting cloud, it seems a substantial storm has settled in for the morning.

Admittedly, I'm slow to accept the obvious: Trust the weather forecast? Perhaps, though it's often unreliable. Or should I never trust a clear sky in the Pacific Northwest? Certainly. Yet, the true lesson here might be that disrupted plans often lead to memorable adventures. Whether it was our hasty retreat to Leavenworth's Enzian Inn or being snug in our van at Fort Ebey during a downpour, each unexpected turn has enriched our lives.

This rain ensures our Mazama trip will be unforgettable. What unfolds next remains to be seen—perhaps the sun will emerge, or maybe we'll relocate to a drier setting. Whatever the outcome, I'm ready to embrace the spontaneity.

In hindsight, while I couldn't pen this book from a rain-soaked tent without cell service, the delay allowed for a richer retelling, as instructed by Eric, my editor. If you find this section overlong, it's thanks to his directive for more detail—intended for a chuckle if it remains in the final edit. Otherwise, Eric, this note's for you.

Thankfully, the weather cleared, and we enjoyed another delightful day of campsite antics. We've returned home safely, with our camping gear now better prepared for any future downpours. Despite my continued skepticism towards weather reports, I've adapted our equipment for greater comfort, rain or shine.

Dogs do speak, but only to those who know how to listen.

Of course I Talk to myself. Sometimes I need expert advice.

28

CHILIN WITH MILLY

I've always dreamed of an experience like John Steinbeck's in "Travels with Charley"—hitting the road and traveling across the country with a poodle by my side. Seeing the sights and meeting people while your dog sits proudly by you is a magical thought. I love road trips, so who knows, maybe this vision will be in my future. Right now, though, I'm living a different dog life.

Despite my love for Steinbeck, it was purely coincidental that I ended up with a poodle. I didn't want a poodle; I didn't even want a second dog at the time. However, Harper wanted a purple poodle, and Lindsey thought that was a great idea. Unable to find a purple one, Lindsey settled for the black variety. I mention Lindsey because despite my objections, she persuaded me into welcoming the poodle into our family.

I was at Moceri Construction about to go into a meeting with some potential clients whom I had never met before. I'm having a hard time remembering all the details, but I think it was three women. We were looking at building out a few adjoining lots. While I'm shaking hands and doing intros, in walks Lindsey, Harper, and another woman I had never met. This last woman had an adorable puppy with her whose preferred spot was to sit on her foot.

As I took in the scene, I knew I was being played and that the outcome was a foregone conclusion. Lindsey assured me of the dog's hypoallergenic nature and insisted it was a great deal, while my three-year-old daughter was falling in love with this little black ball of fur. One of the women I had never met kept telling me what a great dog this was and that I had to get it.

It was quite the scene, and to this day, I think the woman who was pushing for me to bring this dog home was planted by Lindsey. She won't admit it, but why else would she have cared so much. To end the chaos, I agreed and went into my meeting while Lindsey and Harper gleefully departed with our new family member. After wrapping up the day, Hazel, our German Shorthaired Pointer, and I were baffled at how we now had a puppy in our house. While Hazel did draw a little blood the first night when Milly got near her dog food bowl, she and I both had to admit that our new family member was pretty sweet.

From that first night on, Milly stayed away from Hazel's bowl, and they became fast friends as Milly did with most other creatures she encountered. She has this quirky charm about her that is hard to describe. The flutter of her nubby tail and her gentle, yet excited approach makes her irresistible. I have the good fortune that even though I didn't want Milly, it turned out that she wanted me. She quickly became my shadow but unlike Hazel she did it in a subtle way.

Milly excitedly goes on runs with me and is my companion while making trails in the woods. She is sensitive to my personality shifts, sometimes this means cuddling up next to me and sometimes leaves the room. This is usually if things are not going well in a Chiefs game. She barks when someone shows up at the house but is excellent with all people and has a particular affinity for young children and babies. She's even hypoallergenic and doesn't shed. All those are great qualities in a dog, but most of all, Milly is just chill. While she is happy to be active, she doesn't have to be. She just hangs out happy to be a part of whatever is going on. Rarely is she too hyper, and her down moments are few and far between. As someone who is often quite wound up, it is great to have a companion that is so even keeled.

No matter what I'm doing, Milly is chillin' by my side, ready to have a good time. So, while a cross-country adventure sounds like a blast, and Milly would be great at that, for the time being, Milly and I are just chillin'. We go for walks and to the office, we read books and maintain the yard, and at times, although I'm not great at this, we just mill around. Milly is the master of just milling around.

I have learned a lot from Milly; she is a constant reminder to not let life get too stressful. I don't think I will ever get close to Milly's level of chill, but being around her helps me tone it down a bit, and she is eager and ready when I do have my moments of chill. We could all learn a lot from Milly's kindness to others, her positive attitude, and her ability to chill. When life gets you stressed out, or you feel like you are on the verge of burnout, think about Milly and take a moment to chill.

Chilin With Milly

Look around the table. If you don't see a sucker, get up, because you're the sucker.

If you get to thinking you're a person of influence, try ordering somebody else's dog around.

29

DON'T TRUST WIKIPEDIA.

When Lindsey and I were first dating, I didn't understand her ability to persuade through a determined and relentless siege. When she wants something to happen, she subtly sends me links repeatedly until I cave. This often happens with vehicles, as Lindsey loves changing them. It gives me horrible anxiety due to the financial implications of said change, as I'm not a car person. She also does this with vacations, where links to places to go and see keep appearing in our text thread, often without any other comment. After over a decade of marriage, I have built up some resistance to this tactic, although the siege still succeeds at times. It's similar to Superman and Kryptonite. He can handle a little bit of it, but eventually, even his superhuman abilities will falter if exposed to too much. Early in our relationship, about a year in, I had no idea Lindsey was secretly Lex Luthor trying to crush my superhuman ability to make sound, logical life choices. Her first evil plan, bump bump bummm...getting a dog.

At the time, she had moved in with my friend Tony (yes two Tony's) and me, and the three of us were living in an 1100-square-foot, three-bedroom condo. The last thing I felt I needed was a dog. I loved dogs and always planned on getting one at some point, but not then. So, when the subject of a dog came up, I shot it down instantly, saying having a dog in a condo would be a giant pain and not good for the animal. At this point, Lindsey didn't come in with the hard sell, which is part of her strategy. Instead, she slowly kept floating the idea and would occasionally show me a picture of an adorable puppy that would love to have a home. Her next tactic was to add an underling to her supervillain team in the form of Tony. Before I knew it, I was getting it from both sides. My good buddy, who is supposed to always have my back, had been turned. I'm assuming they did this scheming while watching their hours of Saved by The Bell together. He, like Lindsey, didn't go in for the hard sell but has a reassuring way about him that makes things seem like a good idea even if they're not. As they saw my defenses waning, they began going in for the kill. Yes, they understood being in a condo would add a challenge, but there were three of us to care for this animal. We would take turns taking them out, and with all our active lifestyles, it would get plenty of exercise.

Feeling my defenses failing, I got desperate and played the allergy card. I am allergic to dogs, and while that wouldn't prevent me from having a dog in the future, it was simply not possible in the tight quarters. I knew I had overplayed my hand when Lindsey played the hypoallergenic dog card. Now grasping at straws, I explained that I didn't want some little foofy dog and didn't want to spend a bunch of money on this dog. I wanted a normal-sized, normal-looking dog. You see how I went from not wanting a dog at all to now wanting a specific dog? Lindsey's tactics really are impressive. She said OK and seemingly took a step back, then bam! She went in for the jugular.

She subtly threw out the idea of a German Shorthaired Pointer and showed me a picture of one on Wikipedia. They were normal-looking, normal-sized dogs, and it said right there, clear as day, that they were hypoallergenic. I knew nothing of German Shorthairs, and in a moment of extreme weakness, I caved. She and Tony had worn me down. I said that if she could find this dog I had never heard of, we could get one. I figured her finding one was a long shot, and we would stay a dog-free household for the time being.

We were now approaching just a year of dating, and I didn't know that Lindsey's other supervillain power was finding the very thing she wanted. I'm assuming she has some sort of signal similar to the Bat Signal that she sends out, but I still haven't figured out this piece yet. Regardless of her method, within days, one of her minions had found us German Shorthair pups. My dad had passed a sign when driving up to Mt. Baker to go snowboarding and let Lindsey know. The next thing I knew, we were heading up the highway to "check the dogs out," where we would obviously be returning with a puppy.

It was close to Lindsey's birthday, so this made a great present, and I had been duped into thinking I wanted a dog. Now, for those of you who don't know anything about German Shorthaired Pointers, let me fill you in a bit. These are not low-energy, sit-around-the-condo-all-day type dogs. These are working dogs with boundless energy and often severe forms of anxiety. Hazel would have all these traits. This dog simply could not get tired, no matter how far I ran or how many balls I threw. She hated most humans, especially men with beards wearing hats, which described my best friend Casey and every other hipster in Bellingham, so that was great. She also had anxiety in spades, specifically separation anxiety for me. Yes, Lindsey's birthday present decided she could never be farther from me than as far as I could throw a ball.

Hazel's way of coping when I was away was to not cope. She would bark, shriek, break out of crates, and open doors. This dog was the most determined creature I had ever met, and she was determined to be right by my side at all times. With this, the supervillain and her underling had prevailed. They got to live with a dog, enjoying all the cuddling, playing, and petting of the softest ears you have ever felt. The promises of equal duties fell short while I did more than my fair share of dealing with, well, doody. They were especially averse to addressing this need when it happened in the middle of the night. They would take her on runs and walks, but the hours and hours of fetch were on me. None of us were fit enough to wear this dog down on a run.

Not only did I now have this dog that had decided she would accompany me everywhere I went, but there was also one other minor detail that had slipped through the cracks. After Hazel moved in, I noticed my eyes itching just a bit. It was worse when Lindsey let this puppy on my pillow after I went to work. Feeling like something was up, I went back to Wikipedia to check the hypoallergenic dogs list. There was a long list of dogs, but you know what wasn't on the list? German Shorthaired Pointers! To this day, Lindsey swears that not only did she not change Wikipedia, and she would have had no idea how to, had she wanted to. I'm still convinced she had one of her underlings do it.

Hazel would successfully take her high anxiety and pass a good portion of it on to me for nearly fourteen years. She would prove to be the most loyal creature I will probably ever know, and when it was just her, I, and the woods, all was good in the world. When the rest of the world was in the mix, things could become a little dicey, but she did find a few other humans she would enjoy being around, including Lindsey and Harper. Tony did not take his third of the responsibility, but he did welcome her to his home when we wanted to go on vacation.

Hazel lived life in go or stop, and for her, go was fast. This resulted in multiple trips to the vet for stitches or staples and a regular routine of me cleaning out wounds with hydrogen peroxide after she ran into something at full speed. Her worst injury came in the last third of her life while chasing Milly across the street. It was her second time fighting a car, and this one was bad. The vehicle that struck her was going around thirty-five miles per hour. When I saw it happen, I was sure that it was the end, but her incredible determination never wavered. On three legs, that dog ran towards me, hoping I could do something to help her. With her leg dangling and bone protruding, I picked her up and carried her inside, expecting her to die in short order. Instead, I ended up driving her to an animal emergency care facility. I pet her the whole way while she lay in her bed in the front seat.

The facility wasn't open yet when I arrived. There was about an hour gap between when the vet closed and this place opened. As we sat in the dark parking lot, I expected she would die before we could get inside. When we got inside, Hazel was shaking like crazy, and the vets did not think she would make it, but they would keep her overnight and monitor her. Knowing that she would hate being left overnight more than being hit by the car, I reluctantly left her. I went home to finish unloading Christmas presents, which had been the task at hand when she had been hit.

Our family eagerly awaited a call in the morning to see if Hazel had made it through the night and what the prognosis was. I was already surprised they had not put her down on the spot, so I was not optimistic. When the call came in, I nervously answered the phone only to receive surprising news. They had no idea how it was possible, but besides some bruises and a shattered front leg, there was nothing wrong with this dog. They had her splinted, and I could come get her. She would need a lot of help getting that leg back to normal, but she wasn't going to die.

Hazel ended up having a cast over Christmas, followed by a major surgery where her leg would be put back together with the help of some Swedish steel. You can imagine that this procedure and all the associated visits were not cheap. We forked out the money to create a bionic dog because what other choice does one really have? She was too old to lose the leg, and there was no way we were putting her down. Harper won't be able to go to college because we spent the money on Hazel, but we still had this dog Lindsey had manipulated me into getting ten years earlier. After a few months of recovery, which I think Hazel loved because I had to carry her all over the place, she was back to as good as before.

I learned a lot from Hazel. She taught me about loyalty, which I think is one of the most important traits. She showed me that change is possible. For much of her life, she disliked kids to the point that we thought we might have to rehome her when Harper was born. Instead, with a lick on the head, she showed her affection from their first meeting. She never once showed the slightest aggression towards Harper. She allowed her to climb all over her, never doing anything but being her protector. This onslaught of child affection changed her towards all children, never seeming nervous around them again.

She showed me how real anxiety is and that sometimes creatures simply can't help it. There is a wiring in place too strong to overcome. Hazel displayed a competitive nature that would rival the highest-performing professional athlete while showing joy after that drive resulted in her successfully getting a ball over another dog or snatching a frisbee out of the air. She displayed a level of intelligence I had not previously understood in animals. She had the ability to learn and problem-solve, which was incredible. Living with Hazel was not for the faint of heart as she posed challenges at every turn, but what she took in energy, she returned in unconditional love and life lessons. Because of Hazel, I'm a better pet owner and father. I was also exposed to how Lindsey would manipulate me to get what she wanted for the rest of my life. Most importantly, I was taught to always get a second source and never trust Wikipedia.

*The world would be a nicer place
if everyone had the ability to love
as unconditionally as a dog.*

*You give loyalty, you'll get it back.
You give love, you'll get it back.*

30

HAZEL

Watching my old dog unload her bladder.
Few things have made me sadder.
Her days are numbered I can see.
I miss when she ran so free.
Crazy Hazel is her name.
No other dog will be the same.

She taught me lessons before my daughter.
Making me a better father.
As stressful as having her can be.
Many lessons she has taught me.
Missing this dog I know I will.
She will leave a hole that's hard to fill
Scrapes and bruises and many cuts.
This old gal was oh so nuts.

Lindsey said let's get a dog.
She will be your partner on a jog.
Not supposed to affect my allergy.
Wikipedia misled me.
Having a dog would be so grand.
I forgot that we had no land.

In our condo she often cried.
Take me over to the slide.

In Tony's room a box of tissues.
We soon found this dog had issues.
With that nose, a dog for hunting.
But one loud noise got her jumping.
A little stressed, an understatement.
Will the breeder return our payment?

Having Harper we were worried sick.
But with one big sniff and a lick.
Hazel showed she would be so kind.
With this little daughter she eased our mind.

Did not like to come by call.
Unless of course you had a ball.
Chasing Frisbees was her game.
But now her hips oh so lame.

Opening doors and getting out.
These antics really made me pout.
So, in her crate she must stay.
While Milly roams about all day.
Rolling over and doing tricks.
To garner her dog treat fix.

Always excited to chase those sticks.
This old dog really took her licks.
She ran real fast and fought some cars.
Which left her with some awful scars.
Because of the one big whack.
I will never get that money back.
Christmas morning in a cast.

Looking back it makes me laugh.
Thinking back to that little pup.
This wild story sounds made up

For her life there should be cheers.
But instead, I'm expecting tears.
For so long she has been so strong.
Putting her down will feel so wrong.
On the day that she does end.
I will have lost my most loyal friend.

Put her down we had to do.
The time had come I finally knew.
In a box lie her ashes.
Staring at it my heart just crashes.
No more sniffing no more running.
I am seriously bumming.

The memories of this crazy dog.
Linger in my mind, like a fog.
It all started with a trick.
But another dog I would not pick.
Finding more words, I'm not able.
So, goodbye to crazy Hazel.

> *Imagination is more important than knowledge. Knowledge is limited. Imagination encircles the world.*

> *I was trying to daydream, but my mind kept wandering.*

31

CREATIVITY

As a kid, you had creativity.

It's an extraordinary ability.

While we played, we created stories.

Our minds were creation laboratories.

So many ideas, we could burst.

In our own world, we became immersed.

Parents and teachers often scream.

"Why must you always daydream?"

They have forgotten how to be.

A person with a mind that's free.

As we age, we can get more boring.

Instead, we should let our minds keep soaring.

If we want a mind that's wild.

We must find our inner child.

We become our own suppressors.

For a moment, let go of stressors.

A little mind wandering, you will see.

Can unleash some creativity.

They Can't use up creativity. The more you use, the more you have.

The creative process is a process of surrender, not control.

32

CREATIVITY

When our minds are young, we can't help but be creative. Kids love imaginary play; they can create a world from a stick and a cardboard box. You have seen it yourself. While the world is going on around them, a kid can get lost in play. They are in their own world where dragons fly and trapeze artists flip. They can talk to animals and conquer the enemy. These vivid worlds, while yes imaginary, are also real. They are as real in the moment as what may actually be happening around them. They are also real building blocks for the future. We need those dreamers to keep using their imagination if we want to keep coming up with new innovations, solving our world's challenges, and having great stories to read and watch.

I feel like individually we know this, but for some reason, instead of encouraging that sort of learning, what we think needs to happen is to have them learn reading, writing, and arithmetic while sitting in a chair, filling out a piece of paper. I am guilty of putting my daughter in this situation. I am fortunate that she thrives in that world while keeping her incredible imagination intact. It was a challenge for me to be in that environment while my mind wandered off to different places. The result for me was lots of time sitting in the hall because I was being disruptive. I'm not saying I wasn't being disruptive or that I shouldn't have been in the hall. I was disturbing the class, and the teacher needed to do something so the rest of the kids could keep learning. What I am saying is that maybe there is a better way. Maybe we can teach our kids the valuable foundational skills while encouraging creativity.

I am a huge supporter of education and our teachers. The problem I have is the system is set up to teach kids to pass tests instead of teaching them new tools to put their creativity to work. This system is ironic because the whole point of education should be to set kids up to live a successful life by whatever definition they see fit. We are also trying to educate our population so that, as a society, we can advance. By setting up a system that has a goal of turning kids into adults, we are setting ourselves up for missing out on giant dreams that could change the world. I understand that there are teachers and schools that are set up differently that do allow for more of this creativity. That is fantastic. However, that is not an option for most kids, which means we are preventing a large portion of the population in their tracks.

If I look at the high achievers and those coming up with ideas that impact the world, most of the time, it's because they came up with something creative. They used their imagination and creativity to solve a problem or create something new. From the simple to the complex, a bit of creativity ends up having the impact. So, how do we foster this creativity that comes so naturally when we are young yet seems to dissipate as we age?

I think the first piece is facing that reality. As adults, we need to employ more creativity in our own lives to better solve problems. We also need to let kids use their creative minds and encourage the use of their imagination instead of trying to make them like us, boring old adults. To do this, we need to seek out inspiration and give ourselves a chance to be creative. Read a book or watch a movie that takes you to some other world. Play with your kid and let them guide you in a lesson of creativity. Once you remind yourself that this was something you used to do, you will find that your mind wants to go there more often.

By letting ourselves and our children be more creative, we are opening up our world's potential. Problems will be solved, inventions will be made, and new worlds will be created. Embrace and encourage creativity. We are all born with it, and I don't think it goes away, but it can get stifled if we don't use it. Now is the time to foster the growth of that creativity. Use that kid playing in their own world as inspiration for your own creativity and encourage it in them.

Creativity doesn't wait for that perfect moment. It fashions its own perfect moments out of ordinary ones.

Routine is necessary for efficiency; breaking routine is necessary for adaptation.

33

BREAK ROUTINE TO GET CREATIVE

I often find myself doing the exact same routine for days, weeks, and months. The routine rarely breaks, and the aha moments all but disappear. Innovation stops as I go through my routine day in and day out. But when I break that routine, I'm always pleasantly surprised at what comes out of it. Sometimes it is as simple as taking half a day to explore a nearby town. Maybe it is a trip to Maui or camping in the woods. Some of my best ideas have come poolside when my brain is truly free to wander.

Give yourself something new to look at or a different place to read. Check out new businesses, and your creative juices will start to flow. You might solve a problem you have been working through for weeks or come up with a way to streamline a procedure at work. It might give you the motivation to clean the garage or make you more fun when playing with your kid.

Creativity is the key to innovation and problem-solving. Without it, life would be boring. So, give yourself the opportunity to be creative by getting out and breaking your routine.

*We don't stop playing because we grow old…
we grow old because we stop playing.*

*Children need the freedom and time to play.
Play is not a luxury. Play is a necessity.*

34

PLAYTIME

As I have been talking to people over the last couple of months, a consistent theme is that what is important to them has changed from a couple of years ago. They have traded maximizing the dollars they can earn for enjoying what they do every day and who they do it with. Spending time with family was forced upon us, and many realized that not only was it not so bad, but they really enjoyed it. Life is serious, and we have had some serious years, but maybe we don't have to take it so seriously. Maybe we can let go and have fun like we did when we were kids. Instead of focusing on work and seeing if a little fun can come, let's just have fun in whatever we do. That's why I'm saying it's playtime.

Our world is constantly changing, so let's learn from the good and remove the old boring parts. Let's play! Let's play with our friends, family, and, most importantly, our kids. That's really all kids want to do, and we should take a lesson from them. Yes, they will sit and watch TV for hours, but that's because, as adults, we are not giving them, or ourselves, a better option. We have been longing for this opportunity, so don't forget what it's like to not be able to play and return to a normal life of putting the fun on the back burner. Have fun right now in whatever you're doing. Turn it into a game and just play. When your kids want to be silly, don't shoot them down or say you need to do something else. Embrace it and join in the fun.

I'm excited for this new world where people are enjoying life. I'm excited to see people reshaping their priorities. I'm excited to see people make life an adventure, and I'm excited to join in the fun!

It's the things we play with and the people who help us play that makes a great difference in our lives.

It is a happy talent to know how to play.

35

PLAY

The sun is up, so go and play.

This will be a fun-filled day.

Toss a ball, jump in a lake.

Just have fun, for goodness' sake.

There's always pressure to do the work.

And you don't want to come off like a jerk.

But without some play, you will see.

A grumpy person you will be.

Life's too short to not have fun.

Your new approach has just begun.

It doesn't matter what others say.

Ignore the noise, just go and play.

I don't want to grow up, I'm a Toys R Us Kid.

Just play. Have fun. Enjoy the Game.

36

YARD GAME NATION

I love to play, and I love to compete. I get mocked regularly by Lindsey and Harper about asking to play games as if I'm a dog asking to play fetch. "You wanna play a game, come on, let's go play a game, what do you want to play, how about his game, or we could play that, come on what do you say, wanna play?" That's what they say I sound like, but on this point, we will agree to disagree. That being said, I like to play games, so I regularly at least take the room's temperature on the subject.

When I say I like to play, I mean that's really all I want to do. From board games to sports of all types, I'm in, but preferably it's something where there is a winner, and a loser involved because while I love the act of playing, I'm also extremely competitive. Throughout my life, this has taken on many different looks. When I was young, getting my but kicked by my mom in board games, I still always wanted to play. As I got older and Nintendo came on the scene, I spent a couple of decades being into video games in addition to more complex board games. Somewhere in my teen years, I became exposed to foosball, which is probably what sent me down the path I am on today. That and my dad always bought random outdoor toys like Fox Tails and Rocket Balls, which I always loved. There was something to their uniqueness that piqued my interest.

Foosball though is what got me hooked on what I call pub games which evolved into the love of yard games. Some might call it an obsession, others could call it hoarding, but I call it collecting because it makes me sound much less crazy. I was introduced to foosball by my friends Zaq and Jared. The first time I played was in this room above Jared's garage. I had never played before. I think due to just not being around it, but I also remember thinking it was stupid because it was soccer, and soccer was stupid. Not only was that sentiment stupid, as soccer is not stupid, as I would later find out and as most of the world already knew. Just because I didn't understand it, and was not good at it, did not make it stupid. That sentiment was also stupid regarding foosball, as I'm sure we will all agree it is the greatest game ever created in the history of time.

Anyway, so there I was, hanging out with my friends, watching this game I was pretending to be too cool to play when I decided to give it a whirl. Within seconds of playing, my mind was blown. Yes, I sucked but the complexity of how these little plastic men could move the ball around the table was incredible. The sound of the ball ricocheting off the walls and players was nothing short of Mozart's Symphony, and when the ball smacked the back of the goal, the feeling and sound was magical. It has become one of the most satisfying sounds in my life. Now, I had no idea what I was doing. I'm sure my players were flailing about as if rag dolls, constantly out of position. I probably even spun, which is not socially acceptable in the Foosball world.

As we played, Jared proceeded to mop the floor with me, and he did it over and over with the same move. With his three forwards, he would pull the ball towards himself from the furthest away player and strike the ball with authority with the middle forward. It worked every single time. I had no way of stopping it. I just knew I needed to learn how to execute that move. I went home totally hooked. I then got to play at my friend Zaq's house, who had a table in his garage. If I remember correctly, they were borrowing or storing the table for someone else because it was not there when we were younger. After another session, I knew I had to have a table. I was able to talk my parents into getting me one for my birthday, so one August, I believe before my senior year of high school, I got my own table. This was a single-goalie set up, and it had electronic scoring with commentary and flashing lights when someone scored. Remember, this was the late 90s, so when I say commentary, it was the same three or four lines repeated every time, and the robotic voice was staticky. Still fun, nonetheless. This table is still with me today. Aside from it, not going to Washington State University with me when I move the table moves.

The electronic scoring has been replaced with the black slide numbers at each end. Broken men have been replaced, mainly from tables that have been left behind at rental houses. Foosball tables may be the most common left-behind item. The leg broke in the back of Casey's van once, so it is screwed on with a scrap piece of hardwood flooring I had lying around, and I can't even count how many beer spills have been wiped up. For a few years of my life while in college, I played a ton of foosball. Much of it was with Casey, but I would play anyone anytime, and if foosball was an option, that's what I wanted to be doing. There were times when I would get so into a game that my friends would leave me at a party and come back a couple hours later, knowing I would still be posted up with my new best friends playing foosball.

For a while, I got pretty good, but as with all skills, if they are not practiced, they will wane, and I'm sad to say that my former self would demolish me at this point. I probably should be dedicating more time to foosball, but it makes it to the top of the priority list less often than I care to admit. To date, Harper has not found the passion for the game like I have, and Lindsey essentially refuses to play with me. Casey and I still play semiregularly, and I will get the odd game here and there but nothing like those few glorious years where I gladly exchanged a lower GPA for more time at the tables.

Throughout my college years, I was exposed to a variety of games as one would be. At the bar, in addition to foosball, we would play pool and darts. Drinking games were obviously a part of life, and the occasional yard game would pop up at barbecues and such. It was post-college when I really started getting into pub games. I had wanted to eventually have a game room with arcade games in it, but it was obtaining a pool table that really got my brain going. We were going to demolish a house for some customers before building them a custom home, and they said there was a pool table in the basement. I could have if I wanted; otherwise, it was getting crunched with the house. Being the type that says yes to things without thinking about the logistics, I said yes. I figured I would grab a few buddies, and we would throw it in the back of the truck, and that would be that. I was living in a condo at the time, so I'm not sure where I thought I would put it, but that was a problem I would figure out later. Well, when I went down to see this table, I realized I couldn't even pick up a corner. As it would turn out this table was a 1930s-era Brunswick table with massive wood legs and a slate top. This table was awesome, so now I had to have it. I ended up paying a pool table mover to disassemble it and move it to my parent's shop until I had a home of my own to move it to. Eventually, when I got a house, I took what was once the formal living room and put the pool table in there with my Foosball table. This was the beginning.

At this point, I decided I was now a collector of pub games. I started buying them off craigslist, getting a full-size electronic darts game like in a bar and a large shuffleboard table. As my collection grew, I tore down the wall between the formal living and dining room making it all one large game room. Did I mention what a patient wife I have?

It would not take long before my game room was at capacity if I still wanted the space to play the games. This was great, but I was feeling a bit unfulfilled with my game collecting, so I moved on. Well, I added because I will still buy a pub game, often of the tabletop variety, when they come about. Yard games were the next frontier for me. I had the classics like bocce, ladder golf, cornhole, and holey board. I had also acquired a few of the newer ones, like Spike Ball, Kan Jam, and BulziBucket, but I had no idea the path I was about to go down.

For me, yard game's appeal is that they are compact for storage, and I can bring them with me places. Now if I was showing up to a party, I was sure to have a game on hand. The other thing I liked about them was the creativity involved.

I love the idea that a person, or a group of friends, sitting around created a game and then went through all the effort to actually manufacture said game. There is this level of entrepreneurship involved that is so fun.

I began searching the internet for games I hadn't seen before, picking up a few here and there and always checking at antique shops. My collection was slowly growing beyond what most people had when the COVID-19 pandemic hit. I was told to stay at home and wait. Well, sitting around waiting is not my strong suit, so I decided to start the Instagram page Yard Game Nation where I would simply share pictures of my yard games to add a little fun to what was a very unfun world at the time.

What happened after this was incredible. I started discovering more games and interacting with people in the yard game community. Yes, there is a yard game community. It isn't as large as some communities, but it is a passionate fun bunch. I continued to share pictures, played in virtual tournaments, was on the Toss Talk Podcast, and wrote some articles and blog posts about yard games. I also discovered a ton more games that continue to show up on my doorstep regularly.

While learning about all these new games has been a blast, and my collection has grown accordingly, the best part about starting Yard Game Nation has been the connections with people. In a time in which the world was being forced apart, I made friends all over the country in this community. It is the friendliest group of people I have ever interacted with, and how could they not be. They like to hang out, drink beer and play games. But in addition to that, they are creative entrepreneurs bringing their visions to life which is just a blast to watch. It's great to be a small part of it.

The other piece that has happened is I get to share these games. I do it virtually through Instagram and YouTube but also physically with all my friends and family. I introduce new games to people all the time, and I love seeing the responses. I will admit that not all the games I have purchased are created equally. Some have become my favorites, and others leave a little to be desired, but they all represent someone's creation, so I bring them out for people to try. They make gatherings a blast for all ages and abilities, bringing people together in interactive fun. It pulls people away from their screens and gets them moving.

It is great to be reminded that simple fun still exists in a life that can be so serious. That little things and random events can lead to such positive results. The point of my story, and really in creating Yard Game Nation, is to point out how fun life can be. Yes, I think the creativity and entrepreneurship have valuable lessons in them, but the most important piece in it all is to just remember to play and have fun. That is what life should be about, and it is easy to lose sight of that and take things too seriously. So find a game, any game, some friends, and go play.

Growing old is mandatory, but growing up is optional.

We didn't lose the game, we just ran out of time.

37

GAMES

Today is the day to play a game.

I promise you there is no shame.

Behaving as though you are young.

Without a doubt, will be so fun.

Behaving this way, you will see.

Is the action to set you free.

After one has been in prison, it is the small things that one appreciates: being able to take a walk whenever one wants, going into a shop and buying a newspaper, speaking or choosing to remain silent. The simple act of being able to control one's person.

The most important thing is to enjoy your life – to be happy – It's all that matters.

38

BUBBLE WRAP

Growing up, one of the most exciting things that could happen was a package showing up at the door. It didn't happen all that often, and while, more than likely, the package wasn't for me, there was a good chance there would be bubble wrap inside. This meant I was about to experience seconds to minutes of sheer joy, depending on my approach. First, there was the individual popping option that provided prolonged, controlled enjoyment. Pinching each bubble between my thumb and pointer finger created a satisfying pop.

The next option was to lay the sheet of bubble wrap on the floor and slowly walk across it. The pops came fast, but the imperfect shape of the foot meant multiple trips could be had while still finding the occasional pop. If it was a more energetic day, I might dance a little jig on the bubble wrap, the pop-pop-pop being my music as if I were a world-class tap dancer.

To ensure every last pop had been had or to just really get after it from the start, there was the twist method. By grasping the sheet in my hand and twisting in opposite directions, pops would fire off in rapid succession like firecrackers on the Fourth of July. Occasionally, the bubble wrap would show up with the large format bubbles, which was a slight disappointment. They could still be popped with joy, but there were fewer pops, and some would smush around, eventually tearing, never realizing their true potential.

Today, life has changed. With the onset of online ordering, packages now show up regularly. While there is air-filled protection in many boxes, the format has changed dramatically. We now have air pillows protecting the contents, which I have to say just don't provide in the same manner as the small-form bubble wrap. Yes, the loud bang they make when stomped on is fun, but it is short-lived and contains less charm. While I still nostalgically hold on to the good old days, shipping protection beggars can't be choosers, so I'll pop what I can get.

In addition to being really fun, bubble wrap and its imitator, air pillows, are an excellent reminder to appreciate the little joys in life. It is easy to dwell on the big things, waiting for some grand reward. Sometimes they come, but often they are so built up that they are a letdown when they finally arrive. On the other hand, the little things usually come unexpectedly with no build-up, so there are no expectations to be let down. They are just little moments that bring a smile to our face that we can appreciate for what they are.

Hopefully, today you will be lucky enough to stomp on an air pillow. If the shipping gods really feel like blessing you, a package may arrive with some good old-fashioned bubble wrap. Happy popping!

> *Luck is what happens when preparation meets opportunity.*

> *Luck is a dividend of sweat. The more you sweat, the luckier you get.*

39

LUCK

Many people just have good luck,

I must admit that wouldn't suck.

If that life is not your case,

try moving at a different pace.

Preparing for life will indeed,

make that luck guaranteed.

Putting in time before the endeavor,

will make you seem very clever.

Because you chose to do the work,

that result was not a quirk.

The correct moment finally struck,

when preparation turned to luck.

> *I will prepare and some day my chance will come.*

> *If you think education is expensive, try ignorance.*

… 40

GET EDUCATED

I have been investing in real estate since I was twenty years old. It's something I'm really into and has been one of the things I have been most consistent with. I have been continuously learning about real estate since I first dipped my toes in the investing water and have learned that it's a never-ending process.

That first purchase was a four-bed, two-bath, single-family home on a multifamily zoned lot. It was rented when I bought it and purchased at an interesting time. It was 2001, and it was easy to get a loan. The financial crisis of 2008 had not hit, and banks were handing out loans like candy. Rates were right around 6%, and the fact that I worked part-time at the Boys and Girls Club as my only income while I went to college didn't seem to worry the lender. The house was already rented, so they used that income to qualify for the loan. I didn't know anything about real estate, but my Dad had told me that we knew homes, so I better buy one.

That home ended up being a good investment. The appreciation I realized while owning it helped me acquire more homes. I wasn't cash-flowing much income off it because I had a large monthly payment, but I was getting the house for free, and each month I had a little more equity in the home. I don't want to discount that piece because having access to more cash by borrowing against it and eventually selling it was a big help in growing my portfolio.

That being said, the learning that happened with this first property was equally important in my future success. I learned many of the pitfalls of owning a home. I had late-night calls with clogged garbage disposals; apparently, shoving a whole potato down one isn't a good idea. I no longer have garbage disposals in my rentals. I fought with appliances and cleaned up overflowed toilets. I replaced broken windows and painted walls. I learned quickly that owning a rental, especially if self-managed, is far from a passive investment.

I have often been asked why I self-manage my properties, and there are a few reasons. The first reason is that I didn't know any different. I'm not sure I even knew property management companies existed. I had lived in a dorm and owner-managed rentals in my short time out of the house. If I was aware, it was probably a non-starter because of the fee. The rent barely covered my expenses and mortgage, so there was no extra room. The fact that I was working for $8.00 an hour at the time means that I would likely have lost the house had it gone vacant for over a month. As I am about to preach education, there was undoubtedly an element of luck associated with this initial success. I was always able to keep the rent coming in, which was fortunate.

In addition to the maintenance piece, I learned a ton about tennants and property management. I inherited my first tennant'swhen I bought the home. They took good care of the house and paid their rent on time. I'm having a tough time remembering, but I think the next group was pretty good too. At this point, I had no experience, didn't have a good screening process, and knew very little about the leasing process. I was just posting a sign in the front yard and hoping people called. What resulted was a string of tennant'sranging from not great to horrible.

I had one group, which consisted of two guys and two ladies, of which there was one couple. They were friendly young people, and at this point, I had learned that getting co-signers was a good idea if tennant'sweren't paying their own way. They started out great until one of the girls decided she liked the other guy in the house better. This created an extremely awkward situation with, understandably, the now single male wanting to move out. There were altercations as I was trying to collect rent, which never became physical but got close. They wanted to terminate the lease and, on top of it, were short on rent.

I didn't have much in the way of reserves, and missing out on $1,000 of rent was a huge deal. I ended up letting them out of their lease but was having a difficult time collecting the back rent. I called all the co-signers, which is where a big lesson was learned. You see, I was getting co-signers at this point, but I wasn't speaking with them. Upon talking to one of the "co-signers," she told me that she had not signed anything and that her daughter must have forged her signature, so not only would she not be giving me any money, but that I should have her daughter thrown in jail. I once again got lucky as one of the parents had actually signed, and they paid the back rent. The lesson here is to talk to all the co-signers.

I won't go into all the details or stories on this home, but the stories do go on. I unknowingly rented to some drug dealers who moved all sorts of people in and painted walls all kinds of colors without permission. At the time, I wasn't paying for water, sewer, and garbage at my houses, and as it turns out, neither were they. People are often surprised that I take on this expense, but I will tell you from that experience that you really want people to have water, sewer, and garbage. The other piece in my area is that those bills are tied to the property, not the individual, so if the tennant'sget behind on that, it is on me anyway.

I had some other ups and downs on this house and then rented it to a charity that housed homeless youth. I was excited to have what I thought would be a long-term stable tenant and be doing something to help the community. Unfortunately, there was a lack of supervision, and the house was utterly destroyed. I'm talking about someone taking an axe to the walls.

At this time, I had acquired some other houses and was having many more experiences with tenants, both good and bad. I could probably write a whole book about tenant stories, and maybe I will someday. This learning process was extremely valuable for future screening of tennant'sand having improved leases. That being said, it wouldn't have been horrible if some of those lessons had been experienced vicariously through someone else.

While in my early twenties, while getting my hands-on experience, I was also finding ways to educate myself outside of the actual management of the homes. This was pre-podcasts; there weren't many books about real estate, and I hadn't read any of them. I decided to go to real estate school, which was extremely valuable for my career in real estate investing. I had initially gone into it thinking I would become a realtor. However, upon completing the course, I decided that was not a path I wanted to go down. It can be a thankless job with countless hours leading to no income. I didn't want to be on call, and realtors had become partners in my investing and construction businesses. I didn't want to be their competition. I am glad I took the course and highly recommend that anyone getting into real estate investing do the same. It taught me how to speak the language of real estate. It taught me the laws and how to read the forms I was filling out. It gave me insight into what realtors are taught, and not taught, and it gave me the confidence to represent myself as a buyer or seller.

While all this was going on, I also started diligently studying the market. I had my realtor at the time send me every home that came on the market within my parameters. If I drove by a home for sale with a flyer box, I stopped and grabbed one. I would keep these to track how the market was trending. There was no Zillow or Redfin to see the historical sales, and I didn't even know about going to the assessor's page yet. Since then, I have looked at almost every listing that has come on in my area in those parameters and have added to what I buy over the years. The goal in this is simply to know a good deal when you see one.

The other thing I was learning at the time was about financing. This was again trial by fire. I was just saving, putting money down, and getting the best rate possible. What resulted was getting screwed on closing costs by Bank of America and Countrywide. They saw a naive young kid and took advantage. It was my own fault, though. I wasn't educated on the subject and was doing anything I could to try and save a buck on my mortgage payment instead of looking at the whole picture. No one forced me to take the loan, and I could have worked with a local bank that treated me better, but I didn't understand the value at the time.

I had some crazy loans doing the 5-1 ARMs, which was a loan in which the rate was adjustable after five years. These were the types of products that helped create the recession in 2008, and I was eating them up. I had a pile of debt and did not have the income to back it up. If something had really gone wrong with the rentals, I would have been in real trouble. Fortunately, my houses stayed rented. I slowly improved my financial standing and got into better products from a borrowing standpoint.

I would eventually learn about home equity lines of credit and various other loan types, which would prove valuable as I continued investing in real estate. I am primarily a buy-and-hold investor but occasionally sell when the factors make sense.

Today, the world looks completely different since I started investing. There is so much information on websites, podcasts, and books. The learning process can be expedited, and many pitfalls can be avoided. There are investment groups that can be valuable places to learn, which did exist when I started, but I didn't know about them. Now they can be found on social media, and access is easy. There are a lot of real estate mentors and coaches out there. I do some real estate coaching myself. I think this can be valuable. One of my real estate partners learned this way, which was beneficial for him. I would caution that not all of these coaches are created equally, and some can be extremely expensive, offering more fuzzy feelings than tangible knowledge.

If you decide to get started in real estate investing, I still think the number one thing to do, and the most important piece, is to learn the market you will be investing in. Study it religiously so that you know if something is a good deal or not. Markets constantly change in home values and rents and don't always go up. There is so much that goes into real estate investing. I'm not going to cover it all here, but do yourself a favor and get educated to give yourself the best opportunity to succeed.

All of that being said, I'm going to backpedal just a bit. I know I just ranted about how educated and prepared you need to be to invest in real estate, but there is an ugly side to this called analysis paralysis. I talk to a lot of people about real estate casually and in a coaching setting, and it is so common for people to never make a move. They sit on the sidelines, never getting their first deal under their belt. All of my naivety added stress, cost me money and time, but it also allowed me to get into real estate investing. I was young and dumb and didn't know what I didn't know. So, while I think getting educated is essential, and I continue to educate myself daily, don't let that knowledge become debilitating. You are not likely to find a perfect deal, but there are plenty of good deals out there, and that's what you are looking for. You want something that makes sense for you and your goals. Over time, some deals will be better than others, but they all compound and work together as your portfolio builds. So, get educated, but don't let that education be paralyzing. You still need to have the guts to move forward. It is that combination that will have you prepared to pounce when the opportunity arises.

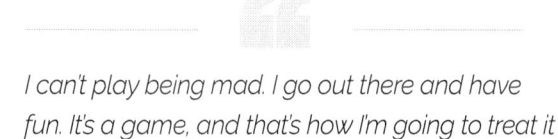

> *I can't play being mad. I go out there and have fun. It's a game, and that's how I'm going to treat it*

> *Do you know what my favorite part of the game is? The opportunity to play.*

41

YOUTH SPORTS

As I write this at 5:00 am on a Sunday morning, I'm two months removed from another season of coaching junior high cross country and in the midst of two basketball seasons. One is my daughter's fourth-grade team, which consists of her and six of her classmates from her small school. The second is that I'm two games into the Mt. Baker Boys high school basketball season. I'm also thirteen hours removed from a memorial for one of my high school track coaches. While I have been thinking about writing about youth sports for a while, I think the latter is what created the inspiration for writing this now.

The coach's name was Mr. Jim Freeman. While he only coached me for a season or two because he retired, he was one of those people who instantly positively impacted anyone he came in contact with. As Lindsey and I sat there at his memorial, she kept pointing out things I do that I must have picked up from him. They were little things like the calf raises I do before every run to warm up that I didn't remember learning from him. But it wasn't something physical he taught me or some secret to winning that was most important. It was the purpose behind coaching, which is to have a positive impact on each and every kid we get the opportunity to coach. The ironic thing is that I had no idea how much he cared or how lucky I was to have had him for a coach, even for a short time, until about twenty years later.

When he coached me, I was a young high schooler who, frankly, was a totally obnoxious goof-off. I would like to say that a lot has changed, but I would probably be called out. I wasn't serious about sports at the time, and I was there more to hang out with my friends and flirt with girls than I was to race. With about sixty students on the track team, there is no reason why Mr. Freeman would have had any reason to give me any attention or even know who I was. So, you can imagine my surprise when twenty years later, he walked up, shook my hand, and said, "Hey Tony, how's it going?"

We were at the Silver Lake Invitational, a meet he had put on for, I'm not sure how many decades. I was there as a high school cross-country coach and was focused on getting our runners ready. I saw him there and wasn't even planning on going up to him because I was sure he wouldn't remember who I was, so I was blown away when he chose to approach me. That thirty-second conversation was more impactful than all the practices and meets when he was my coach. It showed that he cared and fully displayed what a coach's true purpose is: to connect with someone and positively impact them.

Don't get me wrong, Mr. Freeman wanted to win, and win he did with massive success in track, cross country, and girls' basketball, but that's not why he was out there. He was out there to help every kid he could, fast or slow, and knew that by doing so, success would follow. Now that I'm a few paragraphs into this, I realize that an entire book could be written on Jim

Freeman and probably should be, but I am not prepared to do so and am not sure I would be the best person to do that anyway, but I would have been remiss not to include him in this piece.

I have been coaching youth sports for about twenty years, which is hard to believe. It has been a part of who I am for half my life. For nearly that entire time, I have coached at least one youth basketball team, K-8, every year, and in some years, I was coaching two at the same time. I did take a few years off from that when Harper was born. I also coached years of youth baseball and one season of K-1 flag football. The flag football should be a sidebar, except I am now getting to coach one of those kindergarteners as a senior on the varsity basketball team. I have also previously coached high school track, high school cross country, and girls' high school basketball, and I am a few years into a run (pun intended) of coaching junior high cross country. To add to the coaching in this household, Lindsey is a volleyball coach at the youth, junior high, and high school levels and has coached some high school golf.

Through my years of coaching, I have had skill ranges as wide as the Grand Canyon, from those that could hardly run a lap or dribble a ball to the ones that went on to compete in college and a couple that became professional athletes. I should point out that while some I coached continued their sport in college, the professional athletes, both in the NFL, I coached in baseball, basketball, and track, not in football, so I can't take any credit.

By coaching this wide range of skills, I have seen how delusional our society, primarily parents, are about sports.

Most parents think their kid is better than they actually are. It's great to have pride in your child and see them in that light, but it is not great to put unnecessary pressure on the kid to reach a certain level. Yes, hard work can take you a long way, and I think people can work their way beyond their natural ability, but that reach can only go so far. I can tell you that the professional athletes I coached were different physically. Yes, it took hard work and dedication to reach their peak, but they moved differently, even from a very young age, then those around them.

Even competing at the college level is out of reach for most kids, which is why I believe the focus of sports has become so out of whack. From early on, so much attention is paid to having these kids get a college scholarship or go to the league. A small minority will compete in college, some will get a scholarship, and a tiny fraction will go pro. The reality is that those kids will probably reach their potential regardless, so what should we really be focusing on with youth sports?

For me, it all starts with having fun. If kids are not having fun, then no matter what we do as adults, we are wasting our time. Without the fun piece, they will eventually stop and may even come to resent the sport and even us. Once they are having fun, we can show them that we care and that no matter what is happening in life, they know that the coach is there for them and that the coach cares. The next piece is learning that moving their body and exercising is an essential part of life. Humans, on the whole, are an unhealthy bunch that needs to be better at moving more and putting good things into our bodies.

Once we have them out there moving their body and having fun, we can instill what will hopefully be lifelong traits. These are things like being respectful, being a good teammate, and working hard at everything you do. We can then get into the winning piece. Please don't get me wrong. I am extremely competitive and expect to win at everything in life, and I do not hand out trophies for showing up. Teaching a kid to win is important, but we have to walk before we can run, so there is a process to getting to that point. It is also important to put things in perspective. Obviously, winning is fun, and those who win in life enjoy the fruits of those victories, but if we are winning in the wrong way, it can be detrimental to future success.

What I mean by this is there are ways to win in youth sports, especially at young ages, by exploiting your team's strengths and the opponent's weaknesses. The problem with this is that it often comes at the expense of fundamentals and doing things correctly. This may result in a win today but losses in the future because of learning bad habits early on. I am a firm believer that kids should be coached to play the game the right way. It may result in more losses early on as the skills are developing, but I believe that it will result in more wins in the long run.

The final piece in all of this is developing those skills that take an athlete to the next level. When that potential and desire are there, it is excellent, but it should not be the focus from day one. When it is the focus from day one, we set our kids up for failure. Yes, a few will reach the pinnacle of their sport, but if I'm being honest, it's probably not your kid, and if it is, they will probably get there regardless. What is far more common than becoming the best of the best is resentment, the breakdown of the mind and body, and often quitting the sport altogether. First and foremost, the kids need to enjoy what they are doing, and out of that, we can foster so many great life skills both in and out of sports.

As I write this, it seems like a whole book on youth sports is in the cards, but that was not my intention. My intention is to shed some light on how broken our youth sports have become and how the emphasis has become so out of whack. We have become so focused on select teams that we are missing the point of sport. Sport is a luxury humans have from our success as the dominant species. Sports are here to play, have fun, and train our bodies for the rigors of life. Unfortunately, as select teams happen at a younger and younger age, we are eliminating a large section of the population from the sport due to a lack of ability to participate. It may be financial, or it may be that they don't have an adult in their life that can get them to all the places that select sports require.

By putting this out of reach for so many, we often exclude those kids who need it the most. They need to have a positive role model in their life, and they need to move in order to be active, healthy people. They need that something positive in their life, so they don't end up filling their void with negatives and becoming a drain on society. They also may be the next stud who, given the opportunity, can reach great heights in the sport. Again, I'm not saying we can't have select teams and that we can't have good competition. What I'm saying is that by doing it so young, we are doing a detriment to our kids, society, and potentially the sport itself by never seeing those who could have a natural gift.

Along with the select teams comes specialization at such a young age. I think this hurts our kids. Learning to move our bodies and use our brains in various ways is good for us. Kids learn different skills and build other muscles in different sports. They develop different neural pathways in their brains and learn lessons from different coaches. A variety of sports and activities can prevent repetitive use injuries by moving in different ways and on varied surfaces. I am of the opinion that the longer a kid can wait to specialize, the better it will be in the long term. Even if you disagree with all of my other points, understand that kids grow and mature differently, and pigeonholing them into one sport at a young age might end up being the wrong bet. Let their minds and bodies develop and see where their ability and desire take them. Our job is to expose our kids to opportunities and then let them take it from there. Bulldozing their path is not setting them up for long-term success.

I love sports. I love the competition, I love seeing what humans can achieve, and I love to win, but it is important to remember that those are not the reasons for coaching. Those may be the outcomes, but the reason we are coaching is to help each and every kid grow up to be the best person they can be in whatever that ends up being. That may be improving their jump shot or mile time, but for the vast majority of kids, that's not the case. It's teaching them how to work through challenges and interact with others. It's showing them that exercise can be fun and a lifelong endeavor. It's showing them how to behave like a respectful person and win or lose with pride and dignity. It's laughing and playing and making sure that while they are with you, life is positive and good. Most importantly, it's letting that kid know that there is someone who cares and that, no matter what, coach will be there for them.

> *In the end, it's about the teaching, and what I always loved about coaching was the practices. Not the games, not the tournaments, not the alumni stuff. But teaching the players during practice was what coaching was all about.*

> *You've got to coach worrying about the entire team: Whether that gets you a championship or whether that gets you fired. I think it allows you to coach free. You're coaching with freedom because you know you're doing what you think is right.*

42

MORE THAN BASKETBALL

Last night brought the conclusion of the Mt. Baker high school boys' basketball season. Years ago, I had told myself I would never coach high school sports again, at least while my daughter was young. I had previously coached high school track, cross country, and girls' basketball. While I enjoyed the coaching piece, the time commitment had me away from home too much. I switched to coaching junior high cross country and my daughter's basketball team and assumed that would be that. Well, I guess this is why you never say never because, in November, I found myself back in a high school program.

I knew I was biting off a huge time commitment, and I would be facing months of time away from my family, being tired, and not having enough hours in the day to get everything done. I also knew saying no to this opportunity was not an option. Coaching this team felt like it was twenty years in the making. My friend had gotten the head coaching position and had asked, well really told, me that I would be one of his assistants. We had gotten into coaching together in our early twenties when we began coaching his nephew in youth basketball and baseball. During those early seasons on the court, we talked about how cool it would be to coach a high school program together. With that opportunity now in front of us, we had to take it.

In our twenties, the thought of coaching a high school team was all about basketball. We would teach the fundamentals, offensive schemes, and have lockdown defense. It would be basketball, basketball, basketball, and we could not fathom anything more fun. While this season did consist of a lot of basketball, that was not what this season was all about. More than any other season I have ever been a part of, this season was about something more. This season was about learning. It was about putting morals first. It was about connecting with the kids and helping them prepare for the rest of their life. It was about having fun and bringing joy to the game of basketball.

It is only with hindsight that the meaning of this season truly comes to light. Amid some unexpected challenges and trying to win basketball games, there were moments that stood out.

The first thing I noticed was what a kind group of humans these high school boys were. They cared about each other, their opponents, and, eventually, their coaches. They were hilarious, often making me laugh out loud. While we did not win the most games, I would be shocked if there was another team having as much fun. The second moment was when one of the players brought the coaching staff Native American blankets. It is in his Native American tradition to give a gift as thanks. This gift came out of the blue, surprising all of the coaches. We had no idea we were having such an impact and were surprised that a teenage boy could be so thoughtful.

The third moment was on senior night. The seniors wrote us a letter that the announcer read. They thanked us for coaching and expressed their understanding of the challenges we had faced. They showed their unconditional support, which was more than we could have ever asked for.

As I slowly separate from this season and we begin planning for the next, what stands out is that when we start doing something, we don't always understand why. We think we know, but until we are in it, or even past it, the true meaning may be waiting to reveal itself. This season of basketball is a good reminder to go into things with an open mind. The purpose may be different and more important than you think. Let the purpose of your actions reveal itself instead of forcing what you think should happen. The results may be far more impactful than you imagined.

If you bungle raising your children, I don't think whatever else you do matters very much.

You can learn many things from children. How much patience you have, for instance.

43

FEEDING THE COWS

We have a few cows in our field, a couple for beef, and Margaret, who was originally for meat but is now a pet. That is a bit of a story, and I have told parts of it in different writing pieces. Some are on my blog, and some may end up in this book, but since it's not done, who knows what will make the final cut. The long and the short of it is that my dad promised Harper when Margaret was born that he would not butcher her. He thought this young girl, we think she was three or four, would forget said promise. Well, she didn't, and when it was going to be time for her to be butchered Harper was extremely upset. She expected adults to keep their promises. Called out, my Dad spared Margaret and we inherited a cow. Cows are not lone wolves and need to be a part of a heard so in addition to Margaret we have companion cows. Those cows do get butchered, and everyone is on the same page with that.

These cows have become a big part of Harper and I's lives. We feed them daily and ensure their water is thawed in the winter and full in the summer. I'm not a farmer and not that good at even pretending to be one. The winter months are challenging, with no grass in the field and often frozen temperatures. It's a daily task to keep up with all the details. We will forget to plug in the cow water heating element, and one time one of the cows unplugged it, so we end up with frozen troughs. If we are lucky, we can break through the ice; if we are unlucky, we must haul warm water in buckets to melt the ice. We also regularly forget to drain the hose, so with it frozen, we are once again schlepping water or bringing the hose into the house to let it thaw. The list of challenges the icy weather goes on and on. From my truck not blowing heat until it is driven to getting stuck in the snow, the winter months can be challenging.

I was lamenting about some of these concerns to a friend and he asked me to write this piece and for it to be about parenting. He probably wishes I wouldn't have rambled for two paragraphs without getting to any point, but he knows me, so he most likely expected it. So now I'm going to get into why this responsibility, which I didn't plan on having, I prefer to be the farmer's occasional helper than actually being the farmer, has been one of the best things that could have happened as a parent.

I will be candid and say I wanted Margaret to be butchered when we butchered our bull. I was not happy and actually threw a bit of a fit that this was becoming my responsibility. Early on, when Harper and I had taken over, I was huffing around at having to care for this cow when I exclaimed, "Why do I even need to deal with this cow!"

Harper, upset that I was upset, replied, "Because you are my dad."

At that moment, not only did I feel like a real jerk for not realizing that point myself and for making my daughter feel bad, but I also felt proud that I had such a wise nine-year-old daughter. I wish I could say it has been all sunshine and roses since then, but it hasn't. We have had our spats over missed responsibilities by both of us. There are days when neither of us wants to do the necessary chores. In the winter, it means heading out in the dark, cold morning, battling frozen fingers and slippery ground as we tend to our small herd. In the summer, the sticky situation means hay stuck to sweaty brows and often discovering it in places you would never think it could get.

While we both complain, I'm not sure we do anything more valuable in our father-daughter relationship. We have this daily task that, rain or shine, we are completing. No matter what, we have this time together. It's all the hard things I mentioned above but also so many great things. We load up Milly, who would never miss a feeding, and bump some tunes as we drive to the barn. Country music is often the choice, we are pretending to be farmers after all, but we also get the beat up and dance as we complete our tasks. We are greeted by the sound of the barn door sliding and the waft of hay hitting our noses. We are welcomed by our cows, who amazingly can tell time and get the satisfaction of watching them pull big bites out of their freshly filled trough.

The time we spend together doing this is irreplaceable and in addition Harper has learned the responsibility of a daily task and the importance of caring for another creature. She has learned what commitment means and that there are no days off in many aspects of life. I have watched her get physically stronger as she works to move hay bales and hoist the leaves of hay over the fence into the trough. We are often racing to feed the cows and get her to school, so it is not uncommon for her to head off with hay in her hair. She has also learned that meat does not come from the grocery store. It is a living creature that gave its life for us to eat.

While I learn things like patience and to be more proactive because of these cows, it is still Harper calling me out that will be my greatest lesson. These cows gave me a great tool for being a better Dad. By showing up, being present, and leading by example, Harper learns so much about life. I'm not suggesting that everyone go get some cows, but I do think there are ways to parent that can be extremely effective in helping our children develop that may not be obvious. They are subtle in their approach but big on impact. I would encourage any parent who takes the time to read this to find your own "feeding the cows" that you can do with your kids.

David, thanks for prompting this piece!

It was impossible to get a conversation going, everybody was talking too much.

Conversation about the weather is the last refuge of the unimaginative.

44

CONVERSATE

No one really likes the weather.

We just can think of nothing better.

Asking questions that are curious.

Makes conversations more luxurious.

Try to get that persons downlow.

Instead of asking about the snow.

Instead of talking about a puddle.

Bring up something to get a chuckle.

You can always talk about the rain.

Or you could choose to stimulate the brain.

Any easy topic can be the sun.

But may lack some talking fun.

Get creative with your chatter.

And talk about things that matter.

Weather forecast for tonight: dark.

*Everybody talks about the weather,
but nobody does anything about it.*

45

HOW'S THE WEATHER?

Before you start reading this, do me a favor and turn on the weather channel, check the weather on your phone, and take a look outside to see what the weather is doing.

Great! Thanks for doing that. Now you are prepared to have a conversation with someone because it seems like the weather is an extremely important topic for everyone. That or we are just not creative enough to come up with something else to talk about. It is crazy to me that this is the world we live in. It doesn't seem to matter if it's someone we just met or our best friend. For some reason, our default is to talk about the weather. It is obviously an easy topic that we all have in common, but does anyone really care? There are a few times during the year when the weather is very impactful. The rest of the time, it just is. On top of that, as far as I know, we still don't have any control over it.

This is what I would like to propose. Unless you have a wedding coming up or are about to pour some concrete, let's agree to lighten up on the weather talk. We can all stop wasting oxygen and cover topics that matter. Ask people if they have any vacations planned or how their kids are doing.

Maybe they have an interesting project they are working on or just changed careers. At this point, we are so trained to default to the weather I think any other topic will be an improvement. It doesn't have to be earth-shattering or even insightful, just something that is new, and who knows where the conversation will go.

Here are some ideas to get you started:

- New favorite restaurant
- A great book you just read about this guy's wandering mind
- Making soup in a Keurig – yup, it's a thing
- Great hikes in the area
- S'more recipes – I like two Chewy Chips Ahoy with a marshmallow in-between!
- TV shows
- PodCasts
- Sailing off the edge of the earth
- Methods for getting kids to eat vegetables
- Methods for getting yourself to eat vegetables
- Deepest darkest secrets
- Ways to open a bottle without a bottle opener

You get the point. There are infinite topics out there for us all to discuss. If we can all break away from the default even a little bit, just imagine what we might learn. Don't be afraid to give this a whirl. I predict that the people you are conversing with will love this approach. I can't wait to hear what conversation you end up having!

AFTERWORD

Thank you for reading A Wandering Mind. I hope you enjoyed it and were able to take something from it that can assist you in your life. I want to thank Lindsey and Harper for putting up with my wandering mind on a daily basis. I understand how exhausting it can be and let's face it, it's not likely to change. I also want to thank my friends, family, and pets that were included in some of my stories and those of you that were not but have taken the time to wander around with me.

Putting this book together has been an educational endeavor. When I decided to do this, I thought I would write some pieces and hit print. I have learned that it is a much more complicated process than that and to be honest I'm writing this before we have a cover or a layout so who know what else I'm going to learn. My biggest take away from the process is that the writing was the easy part. Sitting down and writing is a relaxing, fun, creative endeavor for me but to take it from that to a completed project is hard and time consuming. Like so many things in life, it's not the specific thing that's the challenge but all the stuff around it. I'm optimistic that when I'm finally holding my completed book that I will feel like the process was time well spent. If not. The next one I write I'll print out, staple it together.

Thank you again for choosing to spend your time with my wandering mind.

APPENDIX A: 'QUOTES'

01. If you don't go after what you want, you'll never have it. If you don't ask, the answer is always no. If you don't step forward, you're always in the same place **– Nora Roberts**

02. The most effective way to do it, is to do it **– Amelia Earhart**

03. I take rejection as someone blowing a bugle in my ear to wake me up and get going, rather than retreat - **Sylvester Stallone**

04. So don't you worry your pretty, little mind. People throw rocks at things that shine. **– Taylor Swift**

05. You may be disappointed if you fail but you are doomed if you don't try **– Beverly Sills**

06. We must accept finite disappointment, but never lose infinite hope. **– Martin Luther King Jr.**

07. When asked, "How do you write?" I invariably answer, "One word at a time. **–Stephen truKing**

08. Follow your passion. It will lead you to your purpose **– Oprah Winfrey**

09. The meaning of life is to find your gift. The purpose of life is to give it away. **- Pablo Picasso**

10. Jump, and you will find out how to unfold your wings as you fall. **– Ray Bradbury**

11. It is the sweet, simple things of life which are the real ones after all. **– Laura Ingalls Wilder**

12. Every pizza is a personal pizza if you try hard and believe in yourself **– Bill Murray**

13. By failing to prepare you are preparing to fail **– Benjamin Franklin**

14. Don't mistake activity for productivity **– Geno Wickman**

15. The more that you read, the more things you will know. The more that you learn, the more places you'll go. **– Dr. Seuss**

16. Have an adventure. Make memories. Do what you love. Learn something new. Have fun make it special. Live life to the fullest. **– Dr. Seuss**

17. Life isn't about finding yourself. Life is about creating yourself. **– George Bernard Shaw**

18. The future depends on what we do in the present. **- Mahatma Gandhi**

19. Do not go where the path may lead, go instead where there is no path and leave a trail. — **Ralph Waldo Emerson**

20. Be like a duck. Remain calm on the surface and paddle like hell underneath. **– Michael Caine**

21. Continuous improvement is better than delayed perfection **– Mark Twain**

22. The road to success is always under construction **– Nick Saben**

23. If it's true that time is money, don't you think the real question is how you should spend it? — **Snoop Dogg**

24. Carpe Diem **– Horace**

25. Yesterday is gone. Tomorrow has not yet come. We have only today. Let us Begin **– Mother Teresa**

26. Know thy self, Know thy enemy. A thousand battles, a thousand victories.**- Sun Tzu**

27. Life is like riding a bicycle. To keep your balance, you must keep moving. **– Albert Einstein**

28. There's no such thing as work-life balance. There are work-life choices, and you make them, and they have consequences **– Jack Wolch**

29. Don't get so busy making a living that you forget to make a life. **– Dolly Parton**

30. I don't think any man is contented when there are things left undone – **John Steinbeck**

31. Time is really the only capital that any human being has and the thing that they can least afford to waste or lose. – **Thomas Edison**

32. True enjoyment comes from activity of the mind and exercise of the body; the two are ever united. – **Wilhelm von Humboldt**

33. We were on a break! – **Ross Geller**

34. Me thinks that the moment my legs begin to move my thoughts begin to flow – **Henry David Thoreau**

35. And into the forest I go to lose my mind and find my soul – **John Muir**

36. Every problem has a solution; it may sometimes just need another perspective - **Katherine Russell**

37. It is health that is real wealth. And not pieces of gold and silver. - **Mahatma Gandhi**

38. To keep the body in good health is a duty... otherwise we shall not be able to keep our mind strong and clear - **Buddha**

39. If you don't know where you are going, any road will get you there. – **Lewis Carroll**

40. Roads were made for journeys, not destinations. - **Confucius**

41. Life is such a great teacher, but I'm such a slow learner – **unknown**

42. Life is about taking chances trying new things, having fun, making mistakes, and learning - **Unknown**

43. Still round the corner, there may wait a new road or a secret gate. - **J.R.R. Tolkien**

44. If everything seems under control, you're just not going fast enough – **Mario Andretti**

45. Nearly all the best things that came to me in life have been unexpected, unplanned by me. – **Carl Sandburg**

46. Life is a succession of lessons which must be lived to be understood. - **Helen Keller**

47. Traveling in the company of those we love is home in motion – **Leigh Hunt**

48. This is how memories are made...by going with the flow. - **Amanda Bynes**

49. Safe driving is no accident – **Bret Pugmire**

50. There's a gentility on the road. A direct or personal question is out of bounds. But this is simple good manners anywhere in the world. – **John Steinbeck**

51. I learn from my mistakes. It's a very painful way to learn, but without pain, the old saying is, there is no gain. - **Johnny Cash**

52. It's good to learn from your mistakes. It's better to learn from other people's mistakes – **Warren Buffett**

53. The best laid schemes O' mice an' Men often go awry. – **Robert Burns**

54. There are certain life lessons that you can only learn in the struggle - **Idowu Koyenikan**

55. Dogs do speak, but only to those who know how to listen. - **Orhan Pamuk**

56. Of course I Talk to myself. Sometimes I need expert advice - **Goofy**

57. Look around the table. If you don't see a sucker, get up, because you're the sucker – **Amarillo Slim**

58. If you get to thinking you're a person of influence, try ordering somebody else's dog around – **Will Rogers**

59. The world would be a nicer place if everyone had the ability to love as unconditionally as a dog. – **M.K. Clinton**

60. You give loyalty, you'll get it back. You give love, you'll get it back. - **Tommy Lasorda**

61. Imagination is more important than knowledge. Knowledge is limited. Imagination encircles the world. – **Albert Einstein**

62. I was trying to daydream, but my mind kept wandering – **Steven Wright**

63. They Can't use up creativity. The more you use, the more you have.

64. The creative process is a process of surrender, not control. – **Bruce Lee**

65. Creativity doesn't wait for that perfect moment. It fashions its own perfect moments out of ordinary ones. – **Bruce Garrabrandt**

66. Routine is necessary for efficiency: breaking routine is necessary for adaptation – **Brett N. Steenbarger**

67. We don't stop playing because we grow old; we grow old because we stop playing. — **George Bernard Shaw**

68. Children need the freedom and time to play. Play is not a luxury. Play is a necessity. – **Kay Redfield Jamison**

69. It's the things we play with and the people who help us play that makes a great difference in our lives. – **Fred Rogers**

70. It is a happy talent to know how to play. – **Ralph Waldo Emerson**

71. I don't want to grow up, I'm a Toys R Us Kid **– Linda Kaplan Thaler and James Patterson**

72. Just play. Have fun. Enjoy the Game **– Michael Jordan**

73. Growing old is mandatory, but growing up is optional **– Walt Disney**

74. We didn't lose the game, we just ran out of time. **– Vince Lombardi**

75. After one has been in prison, it is the small things that one appreciates: being able to take a walk whenever one wants, going into a shop and buying a newspaper, speaking or choosing to remain silent. The simple act of being able to control one's person. **– Nelson Mandela**

76. The most important thing is to enjoy your life – to be happy – It's all that matters **– Audrey Hepburn**

77. Luck is what happens when preparation meets opportunity. **- Seneca**

78. Luck is a dividend of sweat. The more you sweat, the luckier you get. **- Ray Kroc**

79. I will prepare and someday my chance will come **– Abraham Lincoln**

80. If you think education is expensive, try ignorance. **– Andy McIntyre**

81. I can't play being mad. I go out there and have fun. It's a game, and that's how I'm going to treat it. **– Ken Griffey Jr.**

82. Do you know what my favorite part of the game is? The opportunity to play. **- Mike Singletary**

83. In the end, it's about the teaching, and what I always loved about coaching was the practices. Not the games, not the tournaments, not the alumni stuff. But teaching the players during practice was what coaching was all about. **– John Wooden**

84. You've got to coach worrying about the entire team: Whether that gets you a championship or whether that gets you fired. I think it allows you to coach free. You're coaching with freedom because you know you're doing what you think is right.**- Doc Rivers**

85. If you bungle raising your children, I don't think whatever else you do matters very much **– Jackie Kennedy**

86. You can learn many things from children. How much patience you have, for instance **– Franklin P. Jones**

87. It was impossible to get a conversation going, everybody was talking too much. **– Yogi Berra**

88. Conversation about the weather is the last refigure of the unimaginative **– Oscar Wilde**

89. Weather forecast for tonight: dark. **– George Carlin**

90. Everybody talks about the weather, but nobody does anything about it. **- Charles Dudley Warner**